HUGH ROSS WITH KATHY ROSS

ALWAYS
BE READY

A CALL TO
ADVENTUROUS FAITH

rtb
PRESS

Covina, CA

Cover design: 789, Inc.
Interior layout: Christine Talley

Unless otherwise identified, all Scripture quotations taken from the Holy Bible, New International Version ®, NIV®. Copyright ©1973, 1978, 1984, 2011 by Biblica, Inc.TM Used by permission of Zondervan. All rights reserved worldwide. www.zondervan.com The "NIV" and "New International Version" are trademarks registered in the United States Patent and Trademark Office by Biblica, Inc. TM

Names: Ross, Hugh (Hugh Norman), 1945-, author. | Ross, Kathleen, 1948—, author.
Title: Always be ready : a call to adventurous faith / Hugh Ross with Kathy Ross.
Description: Includes bibliographical references. | Covina, CA: RTB Press, 2018.
Identifiers: ISBN 978-1-886653-01-6
Subjects: LCSH Christianity. | Christian life. | Evangelicalism. | Discipling (Christianity) | Cosmology. | BISAC RELIGION / Christian Ministry / Evangelism | RELIGION / Christian Ministry / Discipleship | SCIENCE / Cosmology
Classification: LCC BV4520 .R67 2018 | DDC 248.4--dc23

Printed in the United States of America

First edition

1 2 3 4 5 6 7 8 9 10 / 22 21 20 19 18

For more information about Reasons to Believe, contact (855) REASONS / (855) 732-7667 or visit reasons.org.

Dedicated to our Pastor Dick and Dottie Anderson
and to our dear friend Dave Rogstad

"Few people can bring as much insight on the Bible, science, and Scripture to bear on life and the important questions of life as Hugh Ross. This valuable book will lift the lid on how a serious Christian, who is equally a scholar and a student of life, has learned how to engage carefully, lovingly, and practically with people from a variety of backgrounds. Rather than being intimidated by questions, Hugh helps us to see 'them' (the questioner), to be prepared, and to act in the moment that God gives to us. I am sure you will be enriched, encouraged, and helped by this latest offering from one of our gifted veterans of the faith."

–Stuart McAllister
Global Support Specialist, RZIM

"This book is so engaging that it is hard to put down. And its release is very timely. For decades, Hugh Ross has been a hero to many of us due to his bold stand for biblical truth and the high quality of his writings and lectures. But, after a while, people want to know the person behind the ministry. What is his story and what made him who he is? *Always Be Ready* answers these questions and many more in a satisfying way. It recounts his pilgrimage with warmth and honesty, and it reveals a man who is an evangelist, a lover of Jesus, and a believer in a God who miraculously intervenes in people's lives today. *Always Be Ready* will motivate you to share your faith, it will increase your faith, and it will make you proud to be a Christian. Thanks, Hugh, for writing this equipping and inspiring book."

–J.P. Moreland
Distinguished Professor of Philosophy, Talbot School of Theology, Biola University
Author of *Scientism and Secularism: Learning to Respond to a Dangerous Ideology*

"Part personal testimony and part apologetics primer, Hugh Ross's new book, *Always Be Ready*, will inspire you to *act* as you become the kind of Christian ambassador who can make the case for God's existence and the truth of Christianity. Unlike any other book Hugh has written to date, *Always Be Ready* will give you a peek into Hugh's *personal journey* as it equips you to share the reasons you have for your hope in Jesus."

–J. Warner Wallace
Cold-Case Detective
Senior Fellow at the Colson Center for Christian Worldview
Adjunct Professor of Apologetics at Biola University
Author of *Cold-Case Christianity, God's Crime Scene,* and *Forensic Faith*

"Beyond all the scientific reasons for belief in Christianity, there is an intensely personal side to Hugh Ross, as well. In this volume Hugh emphasizes his pastoral dimension by connecting his head with his heart. Using his own testimony as a backdrop, Hugh provides practical advice on how to share the Christian faith with others. The various angles and aspects provide helpful insights on how the intellectual side of Christianity is linked to our faithfulness in following Jesus Christ. Such an integrated position provides many helpful reminders that apologetics, evangelism, and other ministry all work hand in hand with each other. Highly recommended."

–Gary R. Habermas
Distinguished Research Professor and Chair of the Philosophy Dept., Liberty University

"*Always Be Ready* is a wonderfully balanced book. Ross balances evangelism and apologetics, reason and emotions, story and fact. This book will motivate and equip both experts and novices. I'm grateful for Ross's continued research and production of excellent resources like this, but also his passion for the gospel."

–Sean McDowell, PhD
Biola University Professor
Speaker and Author

"What a great book! Seldom do you find a book that is both highly instructive and truly inspiring at the same time. World-renowned scientist Dr. Hugh Ross tells his own inspiring story of how God helped him triumph over learning differences. He then gives extremely practical advice for using science to defend the veracity of the Christian faith."

–Dr. Richard Land
President, Southern Evangelical Seminary

"Dr. Hugh Ross has a unique ability to bring science and Scripture together in unified witness to the truth of the Christian faith. In this new book he goes even further, inspiring Christians to not only provide good reasons for what they believe, but also demonstrate their faith in living and powerful ways. I highly recommend this book to any Christian who wants to bring the head and the heart together in everyday evangelism."

–Justin Brierley
Host of the *Unbelievable?* Radio Show and Podcast

"Both Christians and non-Christians alike have benefited from Hugh Ross's efforts to show the compatibility between science and Scripture. Here in this unique book, we get a personal glimpse of Ross's own faith journey, the story behind his Reasons to Believe ministry, and how he has shared the gospel with individuals over the decades. This is an engaging and rewarding read!"

–Paul Copan
Pledger Family Chair of Philosophy and Ethics, Palm Beach Atlantic University
Coeditor of *The Dictionary of Christianity and Science*

Contents

Acknowledgments 9

Foreword by Craig Keener 11

1. Ready for What? 13

2. Reasons in Review 19

3. Readiness in the Early Days 31

4. How God Reached Me 41

5. How God Readied Me 55

6. Readiness and "the Gift" 65

7. Ready for Change 71

8. Ready for Anything 91

9. Ready for the Road 111

10. Ready to Fly 125

11. Always Means *Always* 137

12. Readiness Together 155

13. Readiness and Demeanor 173

14. The Readiness Bonus 181

15. Ready for Action 187

Appendix 193

Bibliography 197

Notes 201

About the Authors 209

About Reasons to Believe 211

Acknowledgments

During the years Kathy and I led the evangelism ministry at Sierra Madre Congregational Church, we had no time for book writing. Since launching Reasons to Believe, we've tried to produce books that demonstrate the harmony between facts and faith, science and Scripture, the natural world and the supernatural realm—books aimed at breaking through skeptics' barriers to faith *and* equipping believers with answers to skeptics' challenges. This book is unique. It's written directly *to* you and *about* you, especially about the ways both God and many of you have worked in our life to advance his kingdom.

Some of you are named in this book, as you've allowed us to tell how your stories intertwine with ours. Some of you even provided stories in your own words to enhance the inspirational and motivational impact we've asked the Holy Spirit to create through these pages. We are deeply grateful for your input and that of countless others, too many to name, whose influence is reflected from virtually every page. Pastor Dick and Dottie Anderson, your names belong at the top of the list. Without you, as well as our friends Dave and Diane Rogstad and family, Wayne and Lucy Atkins, Gary and Vicki de Long, the entire Pearson clan, Bob and Joane Miller, Bud and Carole Wunderly, David and Susan Mowen, Cliff and Jackie Stewart, Soozie Reynolds Schneider, Steve and Zana Scheele, Bernard and Leila Marston, Don Richardson, Alex and Pam Metherell, Alan and Barbara Graas, Dave and Gay Brobeck, Mick and Louise Ukleja, Bob and Sherri Shank, Mike and Marlene Phillips, Howard Hugo and Edie Hugo Kirman, Stan and Judi Lennard, Paul and Sharon Broadus, Mark and Mara Clark, these pages would never have been written. Other current board members also deserve mention: Gordon Arbuthnot, Nina Street Dunton, Eric and Marynelle Klumpe, Mark Messinese, and John van Leeuwen. Thanks for the supportive role you continue to play in our life and ministry.

Deep gratitude goes to our editorial team—Sandra Dimas and Jocelyn

King, who polished and refined the draft, Joe Aguirre who procured the fore-word, endorsements, and permissions, and our faithful volunteers, Colleen Wingenbach, who proofed the manuscript, and Gabbie Lewis, who assisted in selection of highlighted quotes. The creative skills of Charley Bell and Richard Silva of 789, Inc., shine from the cover design and those of Christine Talley, Grüv Creative Communications, from the book's interior. We appreciate your talents!

Finally, we would like to acknowledge Diana Carrée and all our other col-leagues at Reasons to Believe. Your support, encouragement, and extra work allowed us to focus on the book when we most needed to. Your service goes far beyond the call of duty. We're blessed to work with men and women who share our passion for providing new reasons to believe in our Creator and Savior.

Foreword

What an encouraging book to read! And what a privilege for me to be invited to write a foreword.

Behind every God-ordained ministry, there is a divinely orchestrated story. If you have appreciated Hugh's insights in other books, you will appreciate getting to know Hugh better in this one.

By their nature, some books can reveal just one side of us. Hugh's other books have often blessed me because of his intellect, his evidence, and his humble readiness to rethink issues or arguments in light of new evidence. He is respectful and gracious to those who challenge him, whether from an atheistic worldview or from a more conservative Christian standpoint. It is hard to spend much time with him in person, as well, and not recognize that he is a genius, as well as someone ready to dialogue in an open and friendly way whether you agree with every point or not. That side of Hugh does appear in this book.

In this book, though, we also get to know more of Hugh's own intriguing story—his testimony. We hear his heart in a special way, passionate to share God's true love with others. His testimony makes clear what anyone who knows him personally can attest: he is a sincere servant of God, and what he teaches is backed by a life of tested integrity in seeking truth and what matters in the eternal long run. God has given him an effective ministry in helping nonbelievers understand and believe the gospel. Whoever he engages, he does so to honor Christ. Sadly, some people who disagree with some of his views have questioned his fidelity to Christ. For any honest person, this book should immediately lay to rest such misplaced suspicions.

Hugh rightly highlights divine patterns in the book of Acts that help us share our faith today by trusting in the God who really is active in our lives. This is not the Deist God who simply wound up the clock and let it run down, but the God who both delights in the creation that he arranged and acts within it as needed to accomplish his purposes. While some things have obviously changed since the events in the book of Acts took place, God himself has not changed, and his desire to reach people with his love has not changed. When we make ourselves available to those who need to hear, we can trust God to work in special ways, and sometimes he encourages us by letting us see his work!

Hugh narrates many of his faith-building experiences in a way that should encourage any believer and invite the interest of a seeking not-yet-believer. He does so to illustrate biblical principles about trusting God as we share our faith. His accounts remind me, and may remind you, of similar experiences of divine orchestration of events as we commit to share the good news about Jesus.

They remind us also that what matters most in light of eternity, what matters most to God, is the well-being of people created in his image, people who can never experience the full wholeness available to them until they are restored to fellowship with the One for whom they were created. We don't need to be defensive in sharing our faith. God has given us the greatest gift of all, not to make us better than others or to isolate us, but to motivate us to demonstrate the same love that he has toward others who have yet to receive his gift. He is already working in many of their hearts and invites us to join his work by doing our part.

–Craig Keener
F. M. and Ada Thompson Professor of Biblical Studies, Asbury Seminary

Chapter 1

Ready for What?

In the neighborhood where I grew up, "Always be ready" meant planning ways to avoid being ambushed by Zeke's gang. In graduate school, being "ready" meant preparing to defend my research findings, which seemed to challenge then current notions about quasars. When I learned to drive at age 27, my instructor warned me to "always be ready" for other drivers' unexpected moves. Today, living in earthquake country (aka Southern California), I must "always be ready" for *the big one.*

All these examples of readiness represent thoughtful, careful mental preparation. Defensive preparation, in these cases. But, that's not to say *all* readiness involves avoiding dangers or hazards. Readiness also involves preparation for positive opportunities and experiences—readiness for adventure, readiness for celebration, readiness to uplift and encourage, and readiness to see the hand of God in action. My goal in writing this book, as in all my other books, is to focus your attention, attitude, and energy on this positive side of readiness. It springs from my personal experience in walking with Christ. More importantly, it springs from the pages of Scripture.

In his letter to Christ's followers scattered across the far-flung outposts of the Roman Empire—Pontus, Galatia, Cappadocia, Asia, and Bithynia—the apostle Peter writes,

> But set Christ apart as Lord in your hearts and always be ready to give an answer to anyone who asks about the hope you possess. Yet do it with courtesy and respect, keeping a good conscience, so that those who slander your good conduct in Christ may be put to shame when they accuse you (1 Peter 3:15–16, NET).

This passage speaks with great relevance to believers today, especially given the way our world views Christians. Much like the earliest recipients of Peter's message, we're often looked upon today with suspicion, as a hostile subculture holding to "strange" beliefs, "strange" behaviors, and a "naive" otherworldly focus. In certain circles, including academia and media, we're viewed with condescension, suspicion, or outright contempt. We're widely considered "haters" and "bashers," in part due to our own careless words and ugly reactions to those we are called to love. Jesus told us we would meet with trouble and opposition for following him. Here in North America, we face nothing like the persecution that erupted under Nero or that believers in many other parts of the world suffer every day.

Notice in those verses that Peter addresses his exhortation not to a specific segment of the faith community, not just to those with a certain "gift of evangelism," saying *they* should be the ones prepared to give reasons for hope in Christ. No. Peter, inspired by the Holy Spirit, writes this passage to *all* Christians within reach of his letter. The context makes this clear. He means you and me, too.

Yes, there is a special gift related to evangelism, and I will mention it in a later chapter. However, Peter's words, here, call *every* believer to be ready to seize the best kind of opportunity imaginable, the opportunity to make an eternal difference in someone's life! I've learned that this readiness brings with it a wondrous reward—the thrill of seeing God's intervention, his fine-tuning, in your everyday, ordinary life. Make that everyday, *extraordinary* life.

A Promise

We Christians talk about having a personal relationship with Jesus Christ, but how *personal* does that relationship seem if we rarely see evidence of the Holy Spirit's directing our path in an eternally purposeful way? We know we are called to be "salt" and "light" in the world. How real does our saltiness or luminous capacity seem if we never experience God's working in and through us to stir up spiritual thirst or shed spiritual light for another person?

Let's face it: We're about as forgetful as the children of Israel during their trek through the wilderness from Egypt to the Promised Land. Even though they had witnessed astounding miracles before and during the launch of their journey, they struggled with doubt and feeling distant from God when they had gone even a short while without seeing his power on display. We need reminders, too, and I can promise, without hesitation, God will deliver them, on one condition.

I'm fully confident in saying that *if* you follow through on the instruction Peter gives—including the *why*, *what*, and *how*—you will surely see "interventions" (aka miracles) so wondrous, you'll know they are expressions of God's supernatural orchestration. You will experience what some of my friends call "divine appointments" with people God has placed in your path to hear good reasons for the hope we have in Christ.

Readiness brings with it a wondrous reward—the thrill of seeing God's intervention.

Heart Check

What I mean by the *why* of Peter's instruction comes from the first part of the passage. If Christ is "set apart" in our hearts, given the highest place over everything and everyone else we value, our life will show that fact. The fruit of the Holy Spirit will become increasingly evident, and the desire to be involved in what Jesus described as a "harvest" in the "plentiful" fields (Matthew 9:37) will become irresistible.

The necessity of this heart check becomes evident in the latter part of Peter's challenge. Peter makes clear that a close connection exists between the *why* and the *how* of our readiness to offer reasons for hope in Christ. If our communication springs from pride in our own knowledge or skills in argumentation, our demeanor will be lacking in the courtesy and respect that spring from a pure heart. If we seek martyrs' credentials—that is, persecution—our conscience will condemn us and render us ineffective.

Before going on to address the *what* of our readiness, let me clarify an important point about the word *you* (or *your*) in 1 Peter 3:15. When Peter speaks of "the hope you possess" (or "your hope," in some translations of the passage), the word is plural, not singular. In other words, he refers to the collective hope that belongs to all believers in Christ. Your feelings of hopefulness on any given day do *not* determine your readiness to give answers to a person who asks you about your deep trust in the promises of God. Our hope is no mere wishful thinking or emotional high. God makes available to us a deep joy that nothing we encounter can ever truly extinguish.

That kind of steadfast hopefulness amid all of life's ups and downs, twists and turns, will definitely evoke questions. And that's what takes the adventure of walking with Christ to a whole new thrilling, as well as challenging, level.

These brief comments on the *why* and the *how* of Peter's exhortation set the table for a more in-depth discussion of the *what*, the reasons for our hope in Christ. In his word studies on 1 Peter, New Testament scholar Kenneth Wuest offers this magnified translation, similar to that given in the Amplified Bible, of verse 3:15:

> Set apart Christ as Lord in your hearts, always being those who are ready to present a verbal defense to everyone who asks you for a logical explanation concerning the hope which is in all of you.[1]

Wuest's commentary on this passage draws out the meaning of the Greek phrase "present a verbal defense." He compares it with a defense attorney's argument, convincing a judge or jury that the charges against his client—in this case, the Bible—are false and should be dropped.[2]

Our hope is no mere wishful thinking or emotional high.

What to Expect

At this point, you need to know more about the book in your hands, what kind of book it is and is not. First, let me tell you it barely (if at all) resembles any of the other books I've written to date. Only one chapter, the one that follows this one, provides scientific content readers have come to expect from me. Still, even this content comes to you in an unusually simplified, summarized form. If you're familiar with *The Fingerprint of God*, *The Creator and the Cosmos*, *Why the Universe Is the Way It Is*, *Improbable Planet*, *Navigating Genesis*, and/or other titles, you'll notice the difference right away. If that's the kind of book you're expecting, you'll likely be disappointed.

Each of these earlier works provided an abundance of research data relevant to the *what* question, the *reasons* question. And I hope you'll refer to them, as needed, when God brings someone across your path who's looking for scientific evidence for the Creator's existence, the reliability of the Bible, and the harmony between science and Scripture. With respect to *Always Be*

Ready, let me suggest three words to help set a more appropriate expectation: Personal. Applicable. Motivational. In some ways, it's a memoir, and in others, an instruction manual. Its single aim is to inspire action, specifically to mobilize ambassadors for Christ's kingdom. My hope is that this book will prepare you in new and unfathomable ways to recognize and seize opportunities to share the reasons for the hope you have in Christ.

Chapter 2

Reasons in Review

Books and other media abound to overflowing today in the category called "apologetics." A few decades ago, not only were the pickings slim in this category, but many Christians scowled at the term itself, as if it means practice in apologizing (not such a bad idea, really). The Greek word transliterated *apologia* in 1 Peter 3:15 refers, as you know, to making a convincing case, literally, "from" (*apo*) "reason" or "logic" (*logia*) for our hope in Christ.

In a rare cultural bubble characterized by widespread acceptance of the Holy Bible as *holy*, evangelism entails minimal *apologia*. Think back to the days (perhaps a few still remain) when presenting certain spiritual laws or steps to peace with God or a bridge illustration provided sufficient basis for embracing Jesus Christ as Creator, Lord, and Savior. Today, as much as ever, we need simple tools such as these to help make the gospel clear. But for the vast majority of people, like those surrounding the believers who first read Peter's letter, Judaism was a foreign religion, and this new sect claimed a certain Jewish prophet and healer to be God, in person, now risen from the dead and ruling from heaven. Why would anyone believe such a bizarre story? How can any secular rationalist or tolerant humanist of today believe it? Why do you and I believe it?

The answer is simply this—because it's *true*. And how do we know it's true, as in accurate, reliable, and trustworthy to a life-and-death degree? Our answer may well include personal experience, even an encounter with signs and wonders, but are these *apologia*? Perhaps you've met, as I have, individuals who have been "transformed" by some counterfeit gospel or "transfixed" by some supernatural power display. These people proselytize, too.

The uniqueness of God's Word sets our faith apart from all others. No other book reveals both the world *around* us and the world *within* us with complete and demonstrable accuracy and consistency. Testable accuracy and consistency. Increasing accuracy and consistency. So, that's where my *apologia* begins. It ends, of course, with the person who rightfully claimed, "I am the way—and the truth and the life" (John 14:6).

For me, a scientist, I find the surprise factor of starting with evidence from science an effective approach to *apologia*. Most people in the world today assume science argues against the Bible, not for it. This misconception pervades popular opinion, even among scientists who accept it by default. (More on this topic in chapter 13.) And this pervasive assumption makes evidence from science all the more effective, whether you're a professional scientist or simply know one or more scientists whose work you can trust. The biggest and most exciting scientific discoveries are those the ancient Bible writers anticipated.

Just for the sake of review and convenience, let me summarize the four sets of discoveries I've found most convincing in my conversations with nonbelievers and skeptics: (1) cosmic origin and features, (2) fine-tuning evidence, (3) life's origin and advance, and (4) humanity's origin. I want to keep them simple enough and clear enough for you to remember and use. (For more detail, more in-depth explanation, and abundant documentation from peer-reviewed scientific literature, I've included a bibliography at the end of this book.) I certainly don't mean to suggest that these are the *only* evidences and answers needed. Responses to such familiar objections as "the Bible has been changed" or "the Bible contains contradictions" or "what about those who haven't heard about Christ?" all have a place in a believer's *apologia*, and all can be accessed via reasons.org as well as in resources made available by multiple other apologists, such as Ravi Zacharias, Josh and Sean McDowell, Abdu Murray, John Lennox, Dallas Willard, Gary Habermas, Nabeel Qureshi, and Norm Geisler, among others.

> **The biggest and most exciting scientific discoveries are those the ancient Bible writers anticipated.**

Cosmic Origin and Features

At the foundation of every culture lies a story, some kind of word picture, about how the universe, the wonders of the sky, the earth, and life came to be. Cultural anthropologists list the Genesis creation account as one among this fascinating collection of over a hundred creation myths, placing it in the sparse *ex nihilo* ("out of nothing" or "out of chaos") category. Few, if any, of these social science scholars acknowledge that the Bible—beyond Genesis—says much more about the origin and characteristics of the universe than any of these other stories, or that its statements can actually be scientifically tested. Most scholars would be offended at the mere suggestion of an attempt to prove or disprove such stories.

That's where the biblical story stands apart. It invites testing. And although Judaism and Islam claim to share the Genesis account, attention to the additional biblical content on creation separates the Christian version of the story from theirs. Here are the key biblical points the Bible conveys about the origin and features of the cosmos:[1]

1. The universe of space, time, matter, and energy began to exist (Genesis 1:1).
2. It did not emerge from within its own space, time, matter, and energy (Hebrews 11:3).
3. It continues to expand from its beginning (Isaiah 40:22, 42:5).
4. It operates according to a set of unchanging physical laws (Jeremiah 33:25).
5. The law of decay (energy degradation or entropy) is pervasive (Romans 8:20–22).

Until the early part of the twentieth century the infinite universe model held sway in the scientific community. This model posited a universe of infinite extent and infinite duration. Thus, it directly contradicted several explicit biblical statements, including the Bible's opening sentence.

The Bible declares in multiple texts that the universe had a beginning, a beginning that includes not only the start of all matter and energy but all space and time, as well. The solution to Einstein's general relativity equations showed a beginning for all the matter and energy in the universe. Astronomers' multiple independent tests and measurements performed over the past century have elevated Einstein's relativity theories, both special and general, to the status of the most exhaustively tested and best proven principles in physics. Their verifications[2] remove any reasonable doubt of a cosmic beginning. Astronomical observations establishing that the universe has continually expanded throughout its history further affirmed its past beginning.

Space-time theorems reveal that the beginning of matter and energy coincides with the beginning of space and time, as well. In other words, they confirm a transcendent cosmic beginning. The two (nontrivial) conditions on which these theorems rest are that (1) the universe contains mass, and (2) the equations of general relativity reliably describe the dynamics (movements) of massive bodies.[3]

While no doubt exists among physicists and astronomers that general relativity reliably describes the movements of massive bodies for the last 99.9999 99999999999999999999999999999999999999999999999999 percent of the universe's history, some theoreticians have speculated that perhaps quantum mechanics dramatically altered the effects of general relativity when the universe was smaller than 10^{-35} meters (smaller than a ten billionth of a trillionth of the diameter of a proton). Based on such speculations, they suggested that time and the universe may be eternal, after all.[4] Recent measurements of distant quasar and blazar images, however, may establish limits on these speculated quantum effects (specifically, the sizes of quantum space-time fluctuations)[5] that would sustain the validity of the space-time theorems.[6]

As for the biblical claim of unchanging physical laws, including a pervasive law of entropy (ongoing decay), astronomers have established their unchanging nature through observations of distant stars and galaxies. Because of the finite velocity of light, when astronomers observe objects at great distances, they are seeing the objects as they were far back in time, when the light left those objects. Thus, astronomers can directly measure the value of the physical constants undergirding the laws of physics, including the law of entropy, at any time in the past simply by observing a star or galaxy at the appropriate distance. By this means, astronomers have established that the laws of physics apply everywhere in the universe and have not changed by any more than one part in a million during the past 12 billion years.[7]

For thousands of years the Bible stood alone in identifying these five features. Today, astronomers and physicists have established the truth of all five.

Fine-Tuning

Apart from intricate, ongoing, intentional fine-tuning of the entire cosmos from its first split second of existence, no one would be here to reflect on our origins. Every lens through which technology allows us to sharpen our focus reveals a greater, not lesser, degree of design precision. Agnostic physicist Paul Davies describes this evidence as "overwhelming."[8] The list that follows offers a few selected examples.

1. The **precise quantities** of the four components of our universe—ordinary visible matter, ordinary dark matter, exotic dark matter, and dark energy—determine the rate at which the universe expands throughout its history. If too rapidly, only gases form and no elements heavier than helium ever form. If too slowly, all the cosmic gas ends up as black holes and neutron stars and the only elements that remain are those heavier than iron. If just right to within 1 part in 10^{56}, they allow for the formation of the galaxies, stars, and planets (what kinds, how many, when, and where) and all the elements essential for life.

2. Only a rare type of **galaxy cluster** would permit our existence. In most clusters, the galaxies are much too numerous, too large, and jammed too tightly together for any spiral galaxy to sufficiently maintain its structure and be sufficiently protected from deadly radiation for long-lasting physical life to be possible. By contrast, our Milky Way's cluster contains just enough dwarf galaxies to sustain the Milky Way's spiral structure, but not so many, so large, or so close as to disrupt it to the point where it cannot sustain advanced life.[9]

3. Only a rare **type of galaxy** has the potential to host life, and an even rarer one to host advanced life. To date, astronomers have discovered more than 100 just-right features of the Milky Way Galaxy (MWG) that make it suitable for our existence.[10] For one, it's a rare "green" galaxy, a perfect blend of blue (new) and yellow (older, yet not as old as red) stars.[11] A galaxy dominated by blue stars would shower its planetary systems with a deadly flaring of ultraviolet and x-ray radiation. Aggressive star formation in a blue galaxy would also cause major disturbances (warps, bends, spurs, and feathers) in its spiral structure, thus destabilizing its planetary systems. A galaxy dominated by red (old) stars would expose its planetary systems to deadly nova and supernova explosions, again showering them with toxic radiation. Red galaxies also lack sufficient star formation to sustain their spiral structure. You can see why the MWG has been called a Goldilocks galaxy.

4. Our **solar system** stands out for many reasons, including the fact that our Sun is no ordinary star. For decades astronomers have scoured the MWG in search of a star sufficiently similar to our stable-burning Sun that it could potentially host an advanced-life-supporting planet and its life-essential suite of just-right companions—other planets, moons, comets, and asteroids, all with fine-tuned features to make advanced life possible. Though they have found many pairs of twin stars,

astronomers have yet to find a star sufficiently similar to the Sun that it could be a candidate to host advanced life on a hypothetical planet in orbit around it.[12] Nor have astronomers found planetary systems resembling ours. They have found nearly 4,000 planets orbiting hydrogen-burning stars, but only one system (Upsilon Andromedae) includes a planet (Upsilon Andromedae e) resembling even one of Earth's neighbors, Jupiter. However, while Upsilon Andromedae e resembles Jupiter's physical features, the Upsilon Andromedae planetary system far from matches the Sun's planetary system. The Upsilon Andromedae system contains two other planets much more massive than Jupiter. The disturbances caused by the masses and orbits of these two larger planets would rule out any chance for life in their system.

5.   The **Earth-Moon system** differs so radically from any other planet-moon combo yet discovered, it may well be unique in the whole of our vast cosmos. What's more, its oddball features are the very things that make it suitable for advanced life. Earth's quantities of life-essential elements such as carbon, nitrogen, potassium, and sulfur, for example—plus the radioactive elements, such as uranium and thorium, needed to sustain plate tectonics and a strong magnetic field—are all anomalous by extremely wide margins.[13] Earth's water content also is highly anomalous. Our planet is neither bone dry nor soaking wet. Earth has the just-right water content, 0.03 percent, to make possible both large surface continents and large surface oceans, both of which are critical for the long-term survival of life.[14]

Moons may not seem uncommon, but the mass of ours compared to the mass of its host planet exceeds the next largest moon-to-planet ratio by fifty times! And it orbits closely. These unique features of our Moon stabilize Earth's rotation axis, and this stable tilt protects Earth from extreme climatic variations destructive to advanced life.

For a planet to be habitable it must lie within a certain range of distances from its host star, a range in which liquid water can possibly remain in all its forms on the planetary surface. For a planet to be truly habitable it must simultaneously reside in eight other known habitable zones: tidal, ozone, astrosphere, the ultraviolet, photosynthetic, planetary rotation rate, planetary rotation axis, and atmospheric electric field habitable zones.[15]

Life's Origin, Survival, and Advance

The world's leading origin-of-life researchers gather somewhere in the world every three years to review the progress of their research. Usually, scientific conferences buzz with the excitement and exhilaration of new breakthroughs and advances. Not these ones. My colleague Fazale Rana and I have attended some of these meetings over the past couple of decades, and the mood is increasingly depressing because of increasingly intractable problems.

For several decades, the textbook explanation for life's origin and history said that vast oceans filled with dense concentrations of prebiotic building block molecules percolated for about a billion years, giving rise to a single simple bacterium from which all present life on Earth has naturally evolved. Origin-of-life researchers now acknowledge that Earth never had this primordial soup of prebiotics. Carbon, nitrogen, and sulfur isotope ratios in rocks dated to the time of life's origin reveal the absence of prebiotic building block molecules in primordial Earth's crust and oceans.[16] A phenomenon known as the oxygen-ultraviolet paradox shows why.

In the very oldest rocks that stand a chance of showing signs of life, we find those signs.

If Earth's environment at the time of life's origin had contained oxygen, that oxygen would have shut down prebiotic chemical pathways. However, if oxygen were not present, nothing would have shielded Earth's surface from the Sun's ultraviolet radiation of such an intensity as to stop prebiotic chemistry. To compound the problem of missing prebiotics, astronomers have failed to detect ribose sugar or any of the amino acids or nucleobases critical for assembling proteins, DNA, and RNA in interstellar molecular clouds.[17]

Origin-of-life researchers also face a significant time problem. Measurements establish that life's origin occurred over a geologic instant, not over a billion years.[18] Commenting on this rapidity of life's origin, evolutionist Niles Eldredge writes, "One of the most arresting facts that I ever learned is that . . . in the very oldest rocks that stand a chance of showing signs of life, we find those signs."[19]

Yet another intractable problem that stymies any natural, as opposed to

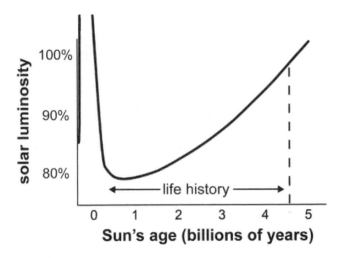

Figure 2: Sun's Luminosity History
The Sun lights up dramatically, getting almost twice as bright as it is now, as it initially gains mass, then dims precipitously during a brief period of mass loss. Then, as its nuclear furnace kicks in, it burns ever more brightly until it expends all its nuclear fuel.

a supernatural, origin of life is the lack of any natural source of homochiral building block molecules. (Chiral molecules are molecules that are manifested as mirror images, where some possess a left-handed configuration while others possess a right-handed configuration. A homochiral sample is one in which all the molecules are exclusively left-handed or exclusively right-handed.) Proteins can be assembled only if all the bioactive amino acids are left-handed in their configuration. DNA and RNA can be assembled only if all the ribose sugars are right-handed in their configuration. Outside of biological systems or their decay products, amino acids and ribose sugars exist as random mixtures of left- and right-handed molecules. Researchers have observed circularly polarized ultraviolet light destroying right-handed amino acids more efficiently than it destroys left-handed amino acids, thereby leaving an excess of left-handed amino acids. They also have shown theoretically that electron antineutrinos preferentially destroy right-handed amino acids.[20] However, natural sources of such radiation, namely supernovae, neutron stars, and black holes, are deadly environments for life and the life-essential components of proteins, DNA, and RNA. Laboratory attempts to produce a pure sample of left-handed amino acids shows that as one approaches purity, the size of the original sample dwindles to zero.[21]

The fact that Earth's first life is not simple presents yet another intractable problem. Scientists now possess evidence that Earth's first life was not a single species of the simplest conceivable bacterium. Rather, it was a complex ecosystem of many diverse microbial species that included highly advanced photosynthetic organisms.[22]

As for the history of life following life's origins, materialists are confronted with the problem of the ever-brightening Sun. Since the time life began some 3.8 billion years ago, the Sun's luminosity has increased by a little more than 20 percent (see figure 2). The fusion of hydrogen into helium inside the Sun's nuclear furnace raises the Sun's core density which, in turn, causes the Sun's nuclear furnace to burn ever more efficiently.

This increasing solar luminosity poses a threat to Earth's life, which can survive only about a one percent change in incident sunlight (and the heat it brings). Life's survival depended on some kind of thermostat. A semi-periodic cycle of extinction events followed by speciation events served that purpose. The extinction events removed life-forms less reflective of sunlight and less able to remove greenhouse (heat-trapping) gases from Earth's atmosphere. The speciation events that followed introduced new life-forms more efficient in removing greenhouse gases and more reflective of sunlight.

This step-by-step sequence kept Earth from overheating and maintained a survivable temperature on Earth's surface as the Sun's nuclear furnace continually increased the Sun's luminosity (brightness). So, in spite of the Sun's 20+ percent brightening, Earth's surface temperature remained optimal for life. However, if nature alone cannot account for even the first life-forms, as simple or complex as they may have been, how can it explain the sudden reappearance of both similar and novel life-forms, increasingly varied and complex life-forms, after each mass extinction event to perfectly compensate for the Sun's increasing brightness?

This step-by-step sequence must be carefully and continually fine-tuned to prevent Earth from becoming permanently sterile. Just-right life-forms in just-right amounts must be removed from Earth at just-right times. The just-right new life-forms in just-right amounts must replace the life that was removed, and at just-right times and in just-right locations. What's more, the epochs between mass extinction and mass speciation events must be brief. (Mass extinction events are events where within a short time period a large percentage of Earth's life is driven to extinction. Mass speciation events are events where thousands, if not tens of thousands or more, new species suddenly appear.)

To sustain life on Earth in sufficient abundance to continue compensating for the Sun's increasing luminosity, the ecological relationships among the species in each mass speciation event must be immediately (or nearly immediately) optimized. All this careful and continual fine-tuning requires a Mind who knows and understands the changing physics of both the Sun and Earth. All this careful and continual fine-tuning requires a Being powerful enough to create quickly and perfectly the just-right life after every mass extinction event.

Design, assembly, fine-tuning, and optimization speak clearly of purpose and personhood. So, to infer the involvement of a personal Creator seems no big logical leap. A growing mountain of scientific evidence suggests that an intelligent, intentional, powerful Craftsperson shaped our universe, galaxy cluster, galaxy, star, planetary system, planet, and moon, not to mention belts of asteroids and comets to make possible an abundance and variety of life on Earth, all for the benefit of human life. Only one written record explains why.

Humanity's Origin and Advance

The evolutionary model for humanity's origin says that the bipedal primates that preceded us (for example, the Australopithecines, *Homo erectus*, and Neanderthals) and we humans naturally evolved from a relatively recent (7.5 to 6.0 million years ago) ancestor in common with chimpanzees. This model predicts that, relative to the currently existing great apes and the extinct bipedal primates, we humans would share many common features, behaviors, and capabilities and few, if any, exceptional characteristics. Furthermore, significant morphological and genetic evolution should be evident within the individual species of chimpanzees, *Homo erectus*, Neanderthals, and human beings.

> **Humans alone ponder the existence and possible attributes of God and show concern about life after death.**

Today, the scientific case for human exceptionalism (the belief that humans fundamentally differ from all other physical life-forms not just by degree but by kind) is strong and growing stronger. Humans alone manifest symbolic capability, and we exhibit such capability at high levels.[23] We can develop and master not just one complex, high vocabulary language, but many. These languages are not just verbal, but written and mathematical, as well. Human beings also have the capacity for rapid and sustained technological advance. Humans alone engage in philosophy, mathematics, and scientific research. Humans alone express curiosity about what lies beyond their accessible environment. For example, what lies beyond the stars and what lies below the oceans, about events long before their existence and events long after their possible existence on Earth. Humans alone ponder the existence and possible attributes of God and show concern about life after death. Humans alone show any evidence of a spiritual nature.

These exceptional features of humans, among many others, show no evidence of evolution. They are just as evident in the most ancient humans that have ever lived as in humans alive today. With respect to morphology, the bodies of humans, Neanderthals, *Homo erectus*, and chimpanzees show no significant evolution (within each species) over the time periods of their (or our) existence. Likewise, we see no significant change in the DNA within each species over the time of their existence.

The origin of human beings, our unique, exceptional characteristics, and the lack of any measurable changes in our physical, intellectual, social, and spiritual features over the course of our existence on Earth fails to fit any conceivable naturalistic model. The scientific evidence points to the supernatural handiwork of God.

Designed for Redemption

In Revelation 7:9, the apostle John writes of his vision, "Before me was a great multitude that no one could count, from every nation, tribe, people and language, standing before the throne and before the Lamb." This verse tells me plainly of a crucial link between God's works of creation and his plan of redemption. At least two verses, 2 Timothy 1:9 and Titus 1:2, state the connection explicitly. God held a specific spiritual outcome in mind before he created anything.

In other words, everything God created plays a role in making possible the redemption of at least a billion human beings. (In the context of first century Greek, an uncountable number would be several sets of 10,000 times 10,000.) To create a planet with the capacity to sustain such a vast number of humans—free-will beings bent on self-destructive autonomy—and to rescue so many of us, through faith in his atoning self-sacrifice, for the eternal splendors of a loving relationship with him, and with each other, requires more exquisite design and management than any earthly mind can begin to imagine. He packed the planet with every resource we would need to communicate this message as widely and clearly as possible before his return.

Personal Implications

If God invested such care in preparing the universe, Earth, and Earth's life to provide a temporary home in which to find and be found by him, why would he not continue to care for the life of every individual human being? If the God of infinite power and love intervened to guide and direct that which has no consciousness, no personality, no emotions, and no spirit, why would he not intervene on behalf of the creatures he endowed with his own image?

Jeremiah 33:19–26 tells us God does not change. Hebrews 13:8 describes Jesus as "the same yesterday and today and forever." Both the Old and New Testament show us God is ready to intervene supernaturally on behalf of people who seek him and whom he seeks. In the next chapter we'll examine biblical examples from the lives of the first Christians—examples intended to set the pattern for all "ready" (and sometimes unready) believers throughout all ages of the church, including ours.

Chapter 3

Readiness in the Early Days

Do you remember the first time you read the book of Acts? I certainly do. I was eighteen at the time and not yet a believer. My first response was to doubt the miracles recorded in that book. How could they possibly have taken place as described? What began to gnaw away at those doubts was my contemplation of the rapid growth of first century Christianity. It defies explanation. Slowly it dawned on me that nothing less than the miraculous events portrayed in Acts could adequately explain the rapidity and extent of the early church's explosive expansion in the midst of extreme persecution.

As a student at the University of British Columbia, I was surrounded by students and faculty who were clearly dismissive of, if not hostile toward, Christianity. I could imagine how they would react if I were to publicly mention my growing conviction that the Bible is true and Jesus Christ really is the Redeemer of broken humanity. Over time, however, it became clear to me that whatever potential ridicule and hostility I might face would pale in comparison to what Christ's followers experienced in the first century.

In Acts I read that the Holy Spirit repeatedly intervened to bring Christ's followers into contact with people already open to receiving the good news of God's forgiveness and acceptance, regardless of the cost. The Holy Spirit also repeatedly intervened to protect, guide, and support these men and women so that they could sustain and continually expand their efforts and opportunities to communicate the good news of salvation through Jesus Christ.

Perhaps if I committed my life to Jesus Christ, he would send the Holy Spirit to guide and empower me in my encounters with people, particularly with those people he would lead me to or bring to me. Gradually, I came to understand that my initial apprehensions were grounded in the mistaken belief that I would be facing people and challenges alone. Reading the book of Acts and beyond made clear that the Holy Spirit would always be right there with me, assisting me every step of the way to complete the good works that God had "prepared in advance" for me to do (Ephesians 2:10), just as he was with Philip, Peter, and Paul, for example.

Whatever potential ridicule and hostility I might face would pale in comparison to what Christ's followers experienced in the first century.

Philip and the Ethiopian Official

Philip's name first appears in Acts 6 as one of the seven deacons chosen to serve the early believers, the Christ-followers who banded together in Jerusalem. In Acts 8, we read that a great persecution broke out against the Jerusalem congregation and, as a result, these men and women and their families—all but a few of the apostles—scattered throughout Judea and Samaria.

In the midst of his successful ministry in Samaria, Philip received a visit from an angel, who instructed him to travel down the road toward Gaza. While on his obedient way, Philip saw an Ethiopian official in his chariot. The Holy Spirit nudged Philip to go toward the chariot and stand nearby. There Philip could hear the official reading aloud from the writings of Isaiah, prompting Philip to ask, "Do you understand what you are reading?" (Acts 8:30).

The portion of the Isaiah scroll from which the official had been reading describes the future sufferings of the Messiah, the chosen one through whom God would make his gift of eternal salvation from sin and its devastating consequences available to all of humanity. Philip's question led to a life-changing conversation. The official understood the text, received God's offer of salvation in Jesus Christ, had Philip baptize him, and went on his way rejoicing in what the Savior had done for him.

Given that this official was the Ethiopian queen's treasurer, a person of great influence in his home country, he most likely played a role in bringing Christianity to Ethiopia. Meanwhile, God had special plans for Philip, too. Instead of returning to Samaria, Philip took the Mediterranean coastal road and spread the story of Jesus's life, death, and resurrection—and what this story means—to all the towns stretching from Azotus (near ancient Ashdod) north to Caesarea.

The account of Philip and the Ethiopian contains several obvious instances of what I would call divine orchestration. First, God allowed a just-right persecution to move the early believers out beyond Jerusalem. Second, that persecution brought Philip to Samaria, a place Jewish people typically avoided. Third, God used Philip to minister to the Samaritans, a people group despised by Jews and at first considered unworthy to hear and receive Christ's offer of salvation. Fourth, one of God's angels appeared to Philip, directing him to leave his burgeoning ministry in Samaria at its peak to travel southward toward Gaza. Fifth, Philip "happened" to meet the treasurer of Ethiopia who "happened" to be reading aloud a passage in Isaiah that "happened" to be the text predicting the redemptive ministry of the Messiah. Sixth, the Ethiopian was receptive to everything Philip said to him, committed his life to Christ, and asked to be baptized, all within a few hours' chariot ride. Seventh, the Holy Spirit suddenly took Philip away from the Ethiopian while the two men were enjoying fellowship and sent them in opposite directions to communicate the good news to more people who had not yet heard it.

A skeptic could argue that any one of these events might happen by pure chance. The combination of all seven, however, given such specific times, locations, and cultural circumstances, seems beyond mere chance coincidence. To me it strongly suggests that God was at work to launch, guide, and expand his kingdom through Philip and an influential foreigner, the treasurer of Ethiopia.

Peter and Cornelius

As much as first century Jews spurned Samaritans, this loathing hardly compared to the degree with which they despised Gentiles. Jewish law forbade association with a Gentile, not even allowing a visit (Acts 10:28). To bring the message of salvation in Christ to Gentiles, God intervened in dramatic and miraculous ways.

First, God sent an angel in the middle of the afternoon to speak to Cornelius, a centurion in the Italian regiment, a Gentile known to pray regularly and give generously to help the poor (Acts 10:4). The angel instructed Cornelius to send men to Joppa to find Peter and bring him back, giving Cornelius Peter's exact location (Acts 10:5–6).

About noon (nap time!) the following day, God gave Peter three successive visions, all on the same theme. In each one, Peter was presented with "unclean" animals and commanded to eat. Peter righteously responded, "Surely not, Lord! I have never eaten anything impure or unclean" (Acts 10:14). To his utter amazement, the voice replied, "Do not call anything impure that God has made clean" (Acts 10:15).

While Peter pondered the meaning of these puzzling visions, the three men sent by Cornelius arrived at the house where he was staying. The Holy Spirit spoke to Peter reassuringly, saying, "Do not hesitate to go with them, for I have sent them" (Acts 10:20). Peter invited the men into the house as his guests, and the next day he, along with several other Jewish believers in Christ, left with them for Cornelius's house.

By the time Peter arrived, Cornelius's home was packed with relatives and friends. Peter explained the message of redemption through Christ's atoning sacrifice on the cross and bodily resurrection from the dead, and all who heard embraced the message. They became followers of Christ and were baptized. Peter stayed on for several more days providing important teaching, empowered by the Holy Spirit.

Some time later, when Peter went to Jerusalem to confront Jewish believers who were skeptical about the Gentiles' having received God's gift, he was able to describe all the extraordinary events whereby the salvation message reached Cornelius's household. Peter's account made abundantly clear to everyone present that Cornelius and his entire household could be considered genuine followers of Christ. The initially skeptical Jewish believers could then praise God, saying, "So then, even to Gentiles God has granted repentance that leads to life" (Acts 11:18).

Fully aware of the long-standing divide between Jews and Gentiles, Jesus challenged his disciples to break through it. Days after his bodily resurrection and before his ascension to the Father, he commissioned them, by his ultimate authority to "go and make disciples of all nations [people groups]" (Matthew 28:19), first in Jerusalem, then "in all Judea and Samaria," and then on "to the ends of the earth" (Acts 1:8).

The story of Peter and Cornelius demonstrates God's participation in the fulfillment of this mission, often referred to as the Great Commission. God prepares a pathway across the cultural and social barriers. He provides the opportunity and the message to those who are ready to step forward.

Paul and Silas and the Philippian Jailer
In some cases, God uses difficult situations, including believers' difficult circumstances, to bring the salvation message to people who would never have

heard it otherwise. For example, in the city of Philippi trouble began when Paul cast a demon out of a tormented slave girl (Acts 16:16–18). This gift of deliverance greatly angered the slave girl's owners, who were accustomed to earning money from the demon's apparent fortune-telling ability. These men created such a stir against Paul and his companion, Silas, that the city's magistrates ordered the pair to be flogged and imprisoned.

The prison jailer was commanded to guard Paul and Silas carefully. So, he put them in the innermost cell and fastened their feet in stocks—taking no chances.

Recovering from the beating that nearly killed them, Paul and Silas nonetheless rallied, raising their voices to pray aloud and sing hymns. Needless to say, their prayers and songs garnered the rapt attention of fellow prisoners.

Shortly after midnight, a violent earthquake struck, so violent that it shook all the prison doors open and broke all the prisoners' chains and stocks. The jailer felt sure that a mass escape would ensue. Knowing that the penalty for allowing prisoners to escape was execution, often by crucifixion, the jailer drew his sword to kill himself.

Paul shouted, "Don't harm yourself! We are all here!" (Acts 16:28). When the jailer saw that what Paul said was true, he

God uses difficult situations . . . to bring the salvation message to people who would never have heard it otherwise.

fell trembling before him and Silas. Throwing caution to the wind, he personally escorted them out and asked, "Sirs, what must I do to be saved?" (Acts 16:30). That night, at his home, the jailer and his entire household received the gift of salvation through Christ and were baptized.

I cannot overstate the drama of what occurred there in Philippi. Roman floggings were so severe that many prisoners failed to survive them, often bleeding to death in the aftermath. Had they not been following the Holy Spirit's direction, Paul and Silas would surely have opted to escape the flogging and imprisonment simply by declaring their Roman citizenship. They chose not to. The Spirit must have assured them something more important was at stake.

Imagine how amazed their fellow prisoners must have been at the behavior of two men placed in the jail's maximum-security cell. They must have been so stunned and so profoundly impacted by Paul and Silas's prayers and hymns that when they had the chance to escape, every one of them stayed put. No one ran.

The jailer most likely heard some of Paul and Silas's prayers and hymns, too. When he witnessed their response to obvious injustice, when he experienced and survived what must have been a terrifying quake, and when he observed the effect of their joyful hearts on all the other prisoners, the jailer could no longer stand. He could only fall at their feet, crying out to become a partaker in a salvation so great.

In the span of less than 24 hours, an unimaginable series of events created a lasting spiritual legacy. In his letter to the Philippians, Paul commends the Christians living there for their partnership in the gospel (1:4–5), obedience to Christ (2:12), their love and joy (4:1), and their generosity in financially supporting the spread of the gospel (4:14–16).

More Interventions

Sometimes, the Holy Spirit guides by blocking plans that seem good and redirecting efforts toward more strategic opportunities than we may be aware of. On their outreach journeys, Paul, Silas, Timothy, and Luke all tried to enter the province of Bithynia, but "the Spirit of Jesus would not allow them to" (Acts 16:7). For some reason unknown to them, they had to spend the night in Troas. That night Paul received a vision. A Macedonian man called to him, "Come over to Macedonia and help us" (Acts 16:9). The next day, Paul and his missionary team headed to Philippi, the leading city of the largest province in Macedonia.

If not for this redirection of Paul's missionary team, the emerging church may have remained in Asia for several more decades. Instead, the Christian faith spread like wildfire throughout the power and education centers of Europe. And it grew in Asia, as well.

The book of Acts describes multiple instances of redirected ministry. What made each redirection possible and successful was the apostles' and disciples' unwavering commitment to the tasks Jesus had assigned to them. They simply never stopped spreading their message and remained always on the lookout for new opportunities to do so. Just as importantly, they trusted the Holy Spirit not only to show them these opportunities but also to provide whatever they would need to follow through.

The Exception or the Norm

Many Bible scholars believe that the book of Acts records a unique period in church history. Acts, they claim, is the account of God supernaturally empowering a choice group of individuals, the apostles and their teammates, whom God ordained to launch the church. I would agree. However, I find no basis in Scripture for concluding that the divinely orchestrated events recorded in Acts are unique and restricted to that first generation of apostles, as some Bible scholars claim.[1] Why would these events not continue through the entirety of the church era to help each generation of Christians reach out to their worlds with the gospel?

No one would question that the apostles were unique individuals, hand-picked as they were in a public manner by Jesus himself. The dramatic nature and number of miracles they performed and experienced seems unprecedented. Nevertheless, a case can be made that much of what is recorded in Acts is intended to be normative for Christians living in all eras until the task the Lord gave us has been completed. The way Luke finishes the book of Acts leaves no indication that a unique period of church history has ended and a new, different one has begun. Readers are left to assume that the acts simply continue.

Acts predominantly describes the mission of the first Christians to bring the news of God's gift of life in Christ to people from every ethno-cultural group they had contact with. Their mission is the same mission Jesus Christ has called *all* his followers to take up. However, throughout all ages of the church, only a relatively few have embraced the mission as their own.

My reasons for believing a change is possible are these:

- God yearns for people to come to him and commissions those who do come to bring others along with them.
- Jesus sends the Holy Spirit to inspire and empower his followers for this mission.
- The Holy Spirit works supernaturally on behalf of those who actively prepare to engage in the mission.
- The book of Acts and other portions of Scripture demonstrate the reality and timeliness of these supernatural assists.
- The experience of Christ's followers throughout the centuries, right up to this day, provides evidence that these supernatural assists are still available and operative.

Therefore, I anticipate that our readiness to engage *ensures* our opportunities to participate in the mission, to complete the work God has prepared in advance for us to do (Ephesians 2:10).

More about Preparation

As I mention in the first chapter, 1 Peter 3:15–16 gives a beautiful, clear description of how preparation enables us to become effective ambassadors of the kingdom. Let's review it again, this time in the NIV translation: "Always be prepared to give an answer to everyone who asks you to give the reason for the hope that you have. But do this with gentleness and respect, keeping a clear conscience."

Theologian and Greek scholar Kenneth Wuest, in his word studies on 1 Peter, interprets this passage as a call to prepare reasonable responses to nonbelievers' reasonable (albeit sometimes antagonistic) questions about our basis for hope: Why do we believe there's a God who cares about us? Why do we accept the Bible as true and authoritative? Why do we believe Jesus is the only hope for humanity? As noted in chapter 1, the wording of the passage emphasizes logic-based, not feeling-based, explanations for our hope in Christ.[2]

Wuest also points out that *you* in the phrase "the hope that *you* have" is the plural *you*.[3] Thus, 1 Peter 3:15–16 implies preparing something more than a personal testimony of how we came to faith in Christ. We're called to offer a reasonable basis for the faith held by all Christians as a corporate body, a reasonable basis for confidence in the Bible's truthfulness and authority, as accepted by the whole body of believers.

The qualifying words in 1 Peter 3:15–16 indicate that a Christian's demeanor in offering reasons proves just as important as the plausibility of the reasons presented. In John 13:35 we read Jesus's comment that nonbelievers will recognize his followers by our love—not only for one another but also for those who don't yet know him and may well be hostile toward believers or toward God, himself. As 1 Peter 3:16 suggests, gentleness, respect, and a clear conscience go a long way to disarming the hostility, contempt, and slander a nonbeliever may harbor or express.

This emphasis on the qualities of gentleness, respect, and a clear conscience may be more important than ever in today's world. Too often I see Christians, including widely known Christian leaders, treat skeptics of the Bible and of our faith as enemies to be defeated and crushed rather than as people for whom Christ gave his life. The pervasiveness of this public response has made today's nonbelievers understandably defensive. They anticipate that Christians will be condemning, condescending, or triumphal toward them. Thus, we have all the more reason to persist in showing compassion, in listening to their hearts as well as their words, and in being honest whenever we have the opportunity to converse.

Book-of-Acts Believers

Anyone who has undertaken any worthwhile endeavor immediately recognizes that effort and practice and more effort and more practice are involved, but passion provides the fuel. So do results. The experience of an encounter that seems too coincidental and too spiritually significant to be anything but God's doing brings overwhelming joy—and multiple blessings. First, it clearly benefits the nonbeliever or wavering believer who listens to the reasons and receives the love we express. Second, it boosts our own faith and character, especially if we're going through trials of one sort or another. Third, it benefits others who may be watching or listening to the encounter, perhaps even watching the long-term impact of the encounter. And, though we may seldom think of this, it also benefits God's angels, who intently observe our interactions on Earth in their quest to understand the mysteries of God's grace.

When I hear a fellow Christian bemoan the rarity of miracles, including evidence of God's personal involvement in their life, I have an idea what's missing. And I have a suggestion for turning things around. It's time to focus some time, energy, prayer, and practice to developing logical reasons, a gracious demeanor, sensitivity to and eagerness for opportunities to answer questions about the reality of hope, and where it can be found. The more active we Christians become in sharing our faith, in preparing and presenting reasons for the truth of Christianity and the Bible, and in developing Christ-like demeanor, the more sensitivity we gain to recognize divine encounters the Holy Spirit has prepared for us.

The qualities of gentleness, respect, and a clear conscience may be more important than ever in today's world.

Why God chooses to communicate his redemptive message through us flawed human messengers may seem as mysterious to you and me as it must be to the angels. But he did choose us for the assignment. We'll explore some of his expressed and implied purposes for such a plan in later chapters, but for now I hope you'll be encouraged to learn how he chose, prepared, and sent a most unlikely candidate as one of his messengers.

Chapter 4

How God Reached Me

When asked to tell the story of how I became a follower of Jesus Christ, I often begin with the surprising fact that I didn't get to know Christians until many years after I became one. That's not to say, however, that during my pre-Christian years God did not work through people, including believers, as well as through the circumstances he orchestrated for me. My hope in offering this detail is simply to demonstrate how significant and effective our prayers and personal interactions can be in the life of people we may never really get to know. If God can bring someone to himself without that person's hearing the good news of salvation in church or in a perfectly polished gospel presentation, why let concerns about imperfection keep you from the joy of participating in God's work?

When I say I didn't really know Christians, I mean I did not get to know any well enough to engage in meaningful spiritual conversations with them. That experience eluded me until about eight years *after* I became a Christian. However, several believers did, indeed, play a critical role in my journey to faith. God also used many non-Christians to get my attention and speak to me along the way.

Why let concerns about imperfection keep you from the joy of participating in God's work?

A Providential Reversal

I was born in Montreal, Canada, forty days before the surrender of Japan ended World War II. My father, a self-taught engineer from Calgary, served the war effort by designing and making hydraulics for Allied aircraft. At war's end, he became one of two partners in a rapidly growing hydraulics engineering firm. During the war, he married a nurse who had come to Montreal from Nova Scotia to be trained and care for the vast influx of wounded combatants.

Dad's plan was to maintain a modest lifestyle while investing the bulk of the company's profits into growing the company. With his technical skills, he took on the role of managing the engineering and production aspects of the firm. His business partner, a venture capitalist, took on oversight of the company's finances.

Within a few years, the business had grown to employ forty engineers and machinists, with the possibility of further expansion as the aircraft industry was booming. That was when my father's partner became tempted by the company's accumulated wealth. Following a carefully laid plan, this man seized the wealth and fled the country, leaving my father with a bankrupt enterprise that had to be dissolved. My father used his own personal savings to give each employee a final paycheck.

With no more than a tenth-grade education and a now ruined business reputation, my father recognized that his opportunity for recovery and for supporting his family were poor to nonexistent in Quebec. So, he used the few hundred dollars he had left to move my mother, my two sisters (ages one and two) and me (age four) to western Canada. We remained for several months with his mother in Calgary while he sought work in the burgeoning metropolitan region of Vancouver, British Columbia. When he landed a (low-paying) job as a machinist in a sawmill, he arranged for the four of us to join him.

One of many important differences between Montreal and Vancouver had to do with my parents' network of friends and neighbors. The people around them in Montreal saw my lack of social, motor, and language skills and became convinced I was "mentally retarded" (a commonly used term at the time). They had been urging my parents to place me in an institution. The immigrant neighborhood in which our sudden poverty forced us to settle in Vancouver was filled with children who, like me, were struggling with language and social development. Autism spectrum disorders were unrecognized and unnamed at that time. No wonder my withdrawn behavior, unexpressive face, extremely limited verbal communication, and lack of normal dexterity led my parents' friends in Montreal to assume I had an intellectual disability.

Memories of my life at age four are quite clear. I understood what people around me were saying, but the few times I made comments, my words seemed to upset people around me. I had no idea why, but to stay out of trouble I trimmed my vocabulary down to "yes," "no," and "cookie." I remember my mother commenting to a friend, "Consider how much Hugh is able to achieve with just those three words."

Perhaps the largest difference between Montreal and Vancouver at that time lay in the realm of educational access. The lack of public schools, then, in Montreal meant my parents would have had to choose either an institution for the mentally challenged, as their friends recommended, or one of the Catholic, Jewish, Protestant, or relatively few (and very expensive) other private schools. In any one of the sectarian schools, I would have been immersed in a monolithic culture. In any one of those schools I would have received religious indoctrination with who knows what negative effects, given the likelihood of exposure to teachers' frustration and peers' ostracism or worse.

Vancouver's public schools in that early post-WWII era were becoming more abundant and ranked among the best, academically, in all of Canada. The immigrant neighborhood in which we settled harbored families from all over the world who, like my parents, had lost their wealth and status, lacked degrees from approved universities, and were starting over. My fellow students and my teachers offered me an exceptionally stimulating educational environment.

Even my birth date proved an educational benefit for me. The war years dramatically impacted demographics. Think about who managed to escape the Third Reich's deadly grasp. Think about who stayed at home, in Canada and the US, to fight in the war away from the battlefields. They were individuals like my dad.

My dad, while still in tenth grade, ranked as the top math student in Alberta's high schools. Because of his unique talents, the armed services exempted him from fighting on Europe's battlefields and instead kept him in Montreal and Halifax to develop and manufacture new aircraft technology. Primarily people like my parents were bearing children during the final year of the war.

Some sociologists and educators identify individuals born in 1944–45 as a unique segment of the pre-baby-boom generation, commonly referred to as the "silent" or "lucky" generation. These were my classmates, unusually intelligent and hardworking. They were the first to come of age during the space race era, the nuclear threat era. Our teachers and professors pushed us harder than perhaps any students before or since to strive for academic excellence, especially in science and math. So, despite being raised in Vancouver's poorest neighborhood, I attended some of the best public schools in the country, populated by some of the top students in the country.

One Special Teacher

In the years right after World War II, the huge influx of refugees from the decimated cities of Europe and Asia caused an extreme housing shortage in Canada. Even so, with three young children to raise, my parents desperately wanted a house of their own, rather than the tiny apartment we occupied in Montreal or the cramped quarters we shared during our first several months in Vancouver. They were committed to finding a way to get a house for our family.

My mother went back to full-time work as a nurse, alternating work shifts with my father to lessen the need (and expense) of childcare. With two incomes and first and second mortgages, they were able to buy a condemned house for $6,000 in what was then one of Vancouver's poorest neighborhoods. We moved in with just six weeks remaining in my first-grade school year.

I was panic-stricken. Although I was failing in all my subjects, my teacher, classroom, and routine at my former school were familiar, and I could fade into the background. Now, this new teacher and new group of kids would see that I was unable to control a pencil to make legible letters and numbers. Because I had learned it's better not to talk, my communication skills were seriously hampered. How would I be able to prove that I could read and do arithmetic?

My new grade one teacher, Lila Campbell, somehow read the fear and frustration in my eyes. With just a few days left in the school year, she held me back after school one day and waited for all the other children to leave. She said, "I am going to ask you questions about these books from the shelf in our classroom. You don't need to talk. Just nod your head for yes and shake your head for no." By this means she determined that I had read and understood the books. She had no way of knowing I had also read *David Copperfield*, a copy of which I found stuffed inside the wall of our dilapidated house.

On the last day of school, Miss Campbell read the names of all those in our class who would pass into grade two. Those not on the list would be repeating grade one. My name was the second to last one she read.

I knew from conversations I'd overheard between her and the principal that Miss Campbell had gone out on a limb for me. I couldn't let her down. During that year's summer vacation I spent hours each day practicing with my pencil, working and working to make legible letters and numbers.

On my first day of grade two, the teacher arranged for us to sit, as far as I could tell, in the order of our grade one academic achievement. I was in the last chair, of course, and my classmates lost no time in labeling me the class dummy. It didn't help—or maybe it did—that I still wasn't talking. But, that very week I resolved that no matter how badly I embarrassed myself or people around me, I would no longer keep quiet. I would take whatever opportunities I had to speak.

After every set of tests in grade two, our teacher reseated us. With each reseating, I found myself several seats closer to the front of the class. By the end of grade two I sat in the first chair. It's tempting to speculate on what was cause and what was effect in this changing arrangement, but school no longer caused me distress, at least not academic distress.

Years later, during a visit to my parents in Vancouver, my mother told me she had been in contact with Lila Campbell. The newspaper had run a story about her retirement after decades of award-winning teaching in the same elementary school. Remembering her with gratitude for her kindness to me, my mother got in touch with her and mentioned that my wife and I would be visiting from California. Miss Campbell responded, "Please tell Hugh I would like him and his wife to come for tea."

Of course, we were pleased to take her up on this invitation. What an amazing afternoon that turned out to be! Over tea and some of the most delicious scones I've ever tasted, Miss Campbell revealed that I was her "mystery" student, the one who most puzzled and intrigued her. She had followed my progression from the bottom of the class to the top in second grade. In fact, from grade one onward she had kept track of my academic progress. She even kept a file of newspaper clippings and reports of my academic career, up to and including my postdoctoral fellowship at the California Institute of Technology (Caltech). What's more, she revealed that she had been praying for me since our meeting back in her grade one classroom. Yes, she was a Christian!

I can hardly describe my joy—and hers—as I let her know I, too, was a believer in Jesus Christ—and that I was using my physics and astronomy education in ministry. She expressed delight to hear that her prayers for me had been answered. She said she had prayed that I would use my education and intellect in service to Christ. Kathy and I had the opportunity to thank her profusely and to praise God with her for the remarkable ways (both known and, until now, unknown) God had used her to shape my destiny. I cannot, nor do I want to, imagine my life's trajectory without the intervention and intercession of this dear Christian lady I had known for just six weeks of my life.

My Parents' Example

Recently, I met a teacher who specializes in working with children on the autism spectrum. She wondered if my parents or any other adult had worked with me during my childhood to understand my initial educational and ongoing social-relational challenges.

My parents, in fact, did the best thing they could have done even without a trace of awareness of autism spectrum disorder challenges. They urged me to back off a bit from my obsessive pencil practice and assured me I would do just fine in school. They recognized I was different from other kids, but they accepted, even respected, my differences, including my honesty. Having observed my aversion to touch, they simply told their friends, "Hugh doesn't like to be hugged." And they decided to ignore the advice of their Montreal friends.

Perhaps the best thing my parents did was to model hard work, resourcefulness, and independence, and they expected no less of me. Their example of independence led my buddy Jim and me to decide we would face down the local bullies, Zeke's gang, all on our own. Being small in size and strength, we relied on our brains to avoid encounters with them, devising intricate plans to outmaneuver them, and we mostly succeeded. I'm not sure our parents ever found out what we went through.

Meanwhile, my father and mother both held down full-time jobs and labored to transform our condemned house into a livable home. Once that transformation was sufficiently accomplished and the second mortgage paid off, my mom quit working for pay and, later, volunteered to work with cancer patients, since she had survived cancer herself. By their words and actions my parents made clear that no matter how far a person may fall, it's possible to make a comeback with solid effort and good cheer. They believed in me. They encouraged and took interest in my endeavors. They never expressed doubt in my capacity to learn or to succeed. In fact, my father used his machining skills to help me assemble my own telescope.

Of course, I had to purchase the telescope parts, first, and that took many years of saving. Early on I collected several hundred empty soda and beer bottles (cash return value of 2 cents and 1.5 cents, respectively) from my neighborhood's street gutters and alleyways, and as soon as I was able I began doing odd jobs for anyone who would hire a scrawny kid to clear overgrown vacant lots, move furniture, mow lawns, trim bushes, or whatever. But that telescope project is a story for later.

Libraries

One of the privileges of graduating into the second grade was gaining access to the school's library. I could even check out books! Within the first few weeks of that school year I read dozens of books on history, geography, and science. One of those books was Fred Hoyle's newly published *The Nature of the Uni-*

verse. In it I read, "There is a good deal of cosmology in the Bible,"[1] and Hoyle described it as "a remarkable conception." This comment piqued my curiosity, but throughout the rest of the book he expressed a thoroughly negative opinion of the Bible and the Christian faith. He rejected what it had to say on almost every issue. Yet, I did not forget his words.

Based on what you know of my peer group, you can guess that I did not appear unique in my appetite for reading. Several of us second graders quickly exhausted the library's collection in our different areas of interest. Consequently, our teacher organized a field trip to the Vancouver Public Library, which at that time had a collection of nearly three million books. She helped us find the bus routes and transfers we needed to get to the library and arranged for us all to get cards to the library's children's section.

After that field trip, I spent nearly every Saturday at the Vancouver Public Library, often reading most or all of a book while there and checking out the maximum five books, typically books on physics and astronomy, to take home. By age eight, I felt certain that my future career

"There is a good deal of cosmology in the Bible."

would lie in some discipline of astronomy. Having exhausted the collection of physics and astronomy books in the children's section, I somehow managed to persuade the children's librarian to trust me with a card for the adult section. When some adults questioned the presence of a child in that section, she went to bat for me. Eventually, I was granted access to the library at the University of British Columbia.

Looking back, I cannot help being amazed that my teacher and parents trusted such a young child to make the trip alone on two buses to the Vancouver Public Library, which at that time was located in a crime-ridden sector of the city, near downtown. The other unexpected circumstance is that Vancouver, which had a population barely exceeding 300,000, boasted a public library with such an enormous book collection, including up-to-date works on astronomy and physics.

Evolutionary Biology Book

When I was ten or eleven, my parents became more than a bit concerned about my now singular focus on physics and astronomy. They encouraged me to read books on other subjects, as well. One day, at considerable financial sacrifice, they purchased "for the family" a thick, illustrated volume on evolutionary biology. They knew I wouldn't be able to pass up the opportunity to read a book we actually owned, and they were right.

As I read, I noted that the book seemed dogmatic in promoting the idea that a simple bacterium naturally arose from a mixture of chemicals in some primordial soup and developed on its own into complex life, including human beings. I was struck by the huge complexity gap between chemicals in the soup and even the simplest imaginable bacterium. How could that gap have been jumped in just *millions* of years? I was struck, too, by the difference in complexity between a bacterium and a vertebrate, especially a human being. How, I wondered, could that gap have been bridged in just a few *billion* years—much less in the *half*-billion years since the Cambrian explosion?

The rate at which the book claimed new species, genera, and families had arisen from the start of the Cambrian era to the advent of humanity by far exceeded the rates observed after the advent of humanity. Here was yet another gap. I remember commenting to my parents, "The numbers don't add up." They shrugged.

The enigma of those gaps continued to bother me. I recall discussing the matter with my high school biology and chemistry teachers. They tried to reassure me that science would eventually provide explanations for the gaps. However, they were unable to even suggest a conceivable pathway by which a possible resolution might come. The books they recommended didn't offer any plausible ideas, either.

For some reason, although my main focus remained on physics and astronomy, I could not ignore the sharp contrast between speciation rates before and after humanity or the complexity gaps between prebiotic chemicals and a bacterium. These bothersome incongruities set me up for the impact of my first significant exposure to Genesis 1 a few years later.

Scientific Method

I don't know whether this was the case in other parts of Canada, but in the public schools I attended, teachers taught and retaught and reviewed the scientific method every year from grade one all the way through to grade twelve. By the time I reached high school, I had been trained to apply the scientific method not only to every science problem I encountered but also to virtually any subject matter open to analysis or interpretation. The scientific method certainly helped me do well in my science classes and win science fairs. It also helped me in my other classes and studies.

Despite all this emphasis on application of the scientific method, none of my teachers provided much background on how and by whom this great tool had been developed. Occasionally they mentioned the contributions of Francis Bacon and Galileo Galilei in promoting the use of this method. Not until many years later did I learn that the scientific method originated and took shape among devout clergymen and theologians who devoted themselves to close and careful study of the Bible's creation texts and of the natural world,[2] which they considered a God-given resource to be studied, understood, and used for the benefit of all humanity.

In my case, God used extensive training in and application of the scientific method to prepare me for my first serious engagement with the Bible. By age seventeen, I had become convinced by my studies in astronomy that an immensely powerful Being, a God, must have brought the universe into existence. Although I doubted a Being so awesome would be knowable by minuscule minds on a small, rocky speck in the vastness of time and space, I thought it only responsible to do some investigation.

I began with what I considered a few reasonable assumptions. First, a Being so capable would certainly communicate, if verbally communicative at all, with perfect consistency. No contradictions would exist between his works in the natural world and his words to humanity, through human reporters. Mysteries may be expected, but no discernible errors of fact or logic. After a search for this Being (described in greater detail below) among the writings of the great philosophers and the holy books of the eastern religions, I picked up a Bible.

The first page of the Bible grabbed my attention. It perfectly followed the scientific method! Genesis 1:2 stated both the frame of reference (point of view) and the initial conditions for the account of six creation episodes, or "days." Immediately I recognized step one of the scientific method, which calls for identifying the frame of reference or the point of view and then step two, identifying the initial or starting conditions. A researcher must make no attempt to interpret or draw conclusions as yet. The third step is to observe and note what occurs when, where, and in what order. I saw the account of the six creation days as an example of this orderly sequence. The fourth step is to note the final conditions and describe how they differ from the starting conditions. At this point and only at this point should the investigator form a lightly held interpretation of the observed events (step five). Then, other experiments and observations can be used to test and revise that initial interpretation, accordingly.

I figured that if the Bible contained other portions describing the origins, features, and historical events of the natural realm, I'd have multiple opportunities to test my understanding of this first page. Thus far, it appeared to accord with what I knew to be the established scientific record. This surprising discovery motivated me to stay up late every night, after everyone else in my family was asleep, to further investigate the biblical texts. Additional fuel came from a few nagging memories.

Street Evangelist

At age ten I had a very brief encounter with a street evangelist. My parents dragged my sisters and me along on their big shopping adventures. Their budget did not include childcare costs. So off we went to a department store in downtown Vancouver. On the sidewalk outside the store stood a man with a Bible in his hand, preaching passionately to all who passed by.

In the few seconds I listened before being whisked inside the door, something the street evangelist said struck home. He said that we all fail to live up to God's righteous standard. In other words, we're all sinners, no matter how good we think we are. I wanted to hear more, but my parents hustled us away from this "zealous nutcase" as quickly as possible.

His words, however, stuck with me and haunted me. They made me question what my parents had taught me about morality, which turned out to be a truncated version of the Ten Commandments: Don't lie, cheat, steal, envy, murder, or commit adultery. They added a few dos, such as be kind, generous, hardworking, responsible, and helpful. They figured that if I could manage these behaviors on my own, I'd be a contributor to the good of society, and that's all, they repeatedly said, any person could strive for. They flatly rejected the notion of life after death.

Oddly enough, a few seconds' worth of sidewalk preaching that I wasn't supposed to hear captured more of my attention and interest than all my mother's many talks promoting her philosophy of life, not to mention the few sermons I heard as a very young child during a brief stint of church attendance. It wasn't just what the street preacher said that impressed me. It was the way he said it and how his words seemed to grip the dozen or so people who had stopped to listen.

The Disunited Church

Having gone to church as a child, my mother considered it both responsible and culturally appropriate to expose her young children to the church's teaching on the Golden Rule and other rules of good conduct. Even so, neither my parents nor anyone else in our neighborhood seemed ready to darken the door of the sagging little church a few blocks from our house—at least not until a charismatic (in personality) young minister was sent there to breathe a little life into the wilting congregation.

Word spread about the lively new minister, and before long the church was packed to overflowing. Being a visual learner with difficulty in auditory processing and feeling uncomfortable in close quarters, I picked up very little of what the pastor said, except that he was against communism. I do remember, though, everyone's excitement when a committee was formed to oversee the reconstruction of the dilapidated church building.

Because my father was known in the neighborhood for his engineering skills and reconstruction work on our house, not to mention his thriftiness, he was asked to chair the building committee. He accepted, and all seemed good until suddenly, without warning or explanation, someone higher up in the church hierarchy reassigned our minister to a new location and sent a different man to take his place.

I was too young at the time to fully comprehend what transpired over the next few months, but my parents later explained. Repeated delays, shortfalls in building material deliveries, and cost overruns prompted my father to check the project's books. Sadly, he discovered evidence that the new minister and the contractor friend he had hired for the job (over the committee's objections) had been dipping quite heavily into the building fund. When my dad brought the evidence of embezzlement to the church board, the board asked him to keep quiet or leave the church.

As you can imagine, that was the end of my family's interest in church. Looking back on my brief childhood exposure to church, I realize God had a different plan for drawing me into a relationship with him. He certainly helped me understand that being in church, even leading a church, did not make a person good. Years later, after becoming a believer in Christ, my childhood church experience made me unusually wary about involvement with church. But, I also realized how God had used this departure from church to protect me. He didn't allow me to be inoculated against Christianity by exposure to a weakly represented version of it, sometimes called "churchianity." Many people I've met walked away from Christ, from what they misunderstood Christian discipleship to be, based on their hollow or even damaging church experience.

A Provocative Proverb

During my growing up years, I heard two Bible verses quoted in my home, but I had no idea at the time they were Bible verses. On a few occasions when I did something to disappoint my father, he responded with a dramatic sigh, "O Absalom, my son, my son" (from 2 Samuel 18:33, KJV). One time and only one time, he uttered these profound words: "There is a way which seemeth right unto a man, but the end thereof are the ways of death" (Proverbs 14:12 and 16:25, KJV). Although I recall nothing about what prompted this statement, I do know I was eleven when I heard it, and it made a deep impression.

> **God had a different plan for drawing me into a relationship with him.**

These words stirred me to question whether I was pursuing the right course in my life. It made me think about death and my eventual exit from this world. It made me curious about the source of my father's words. When I discovered at age seventeen that this thought-provoking proverb came from the Bible, I gained additional motivation to know what else the Bible had to say about life and its meaning.

Several years after coming to faith, I mentioned to my father that this proverb had impacted me deeply. To my surprise, he had no memory of ever quoting it to me, nor did he realize that his words came from the Bible.

Gideon Bible

Sometime during that same year, the Bible came to me again, but in a much different way. Some local businessmen paid a visit to my public school. After checking in with the principal, they entered each classroom, including mine, and placed two boxes on the teacher's desk. They smiled and left without saying a word. The teacher then informed us that there were Bibles in these boxes, and any student who wanted one could come and take one. I'm pretty sure every student in my class went home with a Gideon Bible that day. After all, who in my poor neighborhood would pass up the chance to get a free book?

I put my Bible on the small bookshelf in my room, and that's where it stayed, strangely unopened, for the next six years. However, during those six years, thanks to my English teachers' love of William Shakespeare, I became *almost* fluent in—or at least unintimidated by—the language of King James. So, at age seventeen, when I had become convinced by my studies in physics and astronomy that God must exist, I was able to read and understand the King James Version of the Bible I had received. More on this Bible to come.

An Overheard Conversation

When I was sixteen, a new neighbor moved in just a few doors down the block. Between his house and my family's stood a home that took in boarders. One evening as I was mowing our tiny lawn, I overheard bits and pieces of a conversation between this new neighbor and one of the boarders, who'd been sitting on the front steps, smoking and taking a few nips from a bottle wrapped in a bag.

The neighbor was in the midst of telling the story of how alcohol, cigarettes, and drugs had caused him to lose everything he valued in life and also gave him such terrifying nightmares he couldn't sleep. He ended by saying, "Jesus rescued me from a life of hell on Earth." The boarder seemed skeptical. He demanded tangible proof that the Bible was true and not just a bunch of made-up stories. The neighbor responded by making reference to fulfilled prophecies concerning Jesus and about the rebirth of the nation of Israel.

I didn't hear much of this conversation, but what I heard stirred my curiosity. *Does the Bible really possess predictive power?* I wondered. The stage had been set for a genuine and thorough inquiry, an investigation that would alter the course of my life. As you know, stages don't set themselves.

Chapter 5

How God Readied Me

God used a seventeen-year convergence of unusual and, in some cases, highly unlikely circumstances to prepare me for the ultimate quest: an inquiry into how the universe and life came to exist. Frankly, I felt skeptical about the possibility of finding answers in either philosophy or religion. However, one of my high school teachers had told me if I ever wanted to understand world history or current events, I would need some grasp of both. With his nudge, I felt free to begin my inquiry more for intellectual satisfaction than for any personal reasons or felt needs.

After all, my life was going well. The Joe Berg Foundation's Science Seminars I'd been chosen to participate in during my last three years of high school exposed me to weekly lectures from Canada's premier scientists. I took a leadership position as Director of Observations in the Vancouver chapter of the Royal Astronomical Society of Canada, a role that involved giving public lectures on astronomy. I had won the Grand Award at the British Columbia Science Fair and honorable mention at the Canada-Wide Science Fair for my research on *T Tauri* variable stars. I had graduated with honors and earned a scholarship to the university of my choice, the University of British Columbia. I'd already set my sights on a doctoral program in astronomy at the University of Toronto. Even my need of a summer job had been met. So, I took some time, at last, to read outside what my classes required.

Cosmic Beginnings

As I mentioned previously, my reading in cosmology had already persuaded me, by age sixteen, that the universe had a beginning. A cosmic beginning implies, by no great stretch of logic, the necessity of a Beginner. Given that astronomers frequently referred to Immanuel Kant as the father of cosmology, I considered Kant's books, especially his *Critique of Pure Reason*, a good place to start.

I dived in headfirst, and soon scraped my head. Kant devoted much of the book to discounting any cosmological evidence for God. His approach called for chopping up the cosmological evidence into tiny pieces and subsequently demonstrating that each tiny piece, by itself, provided insufficient proof for God. This line of reasoning seemed to me disingenuous. What's more, Kant's assumption that God would be subject to space and time, rather than vice versa, violated the whole notion of a cosmic beginning/ Beginner relationship. Constraining the Beginner's operations to eternally existent space and time dimensions seemed to me to make space and time greater than the Beginner.

A cosmic beginning implies . . . the necessity of a Beginner.

Putting aside Kant, I picked up the works of other highly regarded philosophers. None brought me any closer to an explanation of the realities observed and measured through increasingly powerful instruments, realities of a transcendent cosmic origin and ongoing fine-tuning for even the possibility of a planet like Earth and its panoply of life-forms. I found them just as disappointing as Kant's books. They seemed to raise more questions than they answered, questions I wasn't asking.

At this point, I was almost convinced I would be compelled to live with the mysterious unknown, perhaps unknowable, at least until technological advances allowed more in-depth probing into the origin and nature of the cosmos. For fun, I read a book of creation stories from many different cultures of the world. They seemed colorful and intriguing, but also more fantasy than factual. Nevertheless, I felt that to be thorough and fair-minded, I should look into the great "holy books" and commentaries of the world's great religions. Perhaps each one held some element of truth that, when combined, would present a coherent picture.

Picking up one after another, I found some wise words about one topic or another, but I also encountered vague, esoteric language and violations of confirmed fact, in some cases, outright rejection of material reality. My greatest disappointment came from finding so much repetition and so little material that could be tested for veracity. I realized, too, the falsehood of the popular notion that all religions are basically the same and equally valid in pointing people to God. That's not to say I would favor restricting religious freedom. After all, that freedom allowed me the opportunity to enrich my understanding of people and culture.

Finally, more than halfway through my seventeenth year, I got around to picking up the Gideon Bible that had been collecting dust on my bookshelf for the past six years. Again, thanks to my teachers' love of Shakespeare, I had no trouble understanding its archaic English. And, as I mentioned in the previous chapter, the scientific method leapt out from the very first page. Not only did the opening declaration and then the chronological overview of Earth's and life's development fit with known science, but also the text provided an answer to the fossil record enigma that had bothered me for years.

This enigma—the appearance of abundant new species, genera, families, orders, and classes of life before the arrival of humanity and not after—finds an explanation in the Creator's purpose and plan for humanity. For six prehuman creation periods, God supernaturally intervened to prepare the environment and create new life-forms for the ultimate benefit of human life. Then, during the seventh "day" (the human era), God ceased from creating new kinds of life to focus on the one creature made uniquely for relationship with a transcendent Being. The mystery of life's very early origin on Earth and of the rapid emergence of increasingly complex life from the Cambrian explosion right up to the appearance of humanity found resolution in the possibility of supernatural intervention. And that possibility is rooted in the reality of a transcendent cosmic origin, which my astrophysical research had been pointing toward for some time.

I spent the next eighteen months testing all the Bible's statements relevant to science, history, and geography. The text gave me much content to test and even encouraged testing (1 Thessalonians 5:21). That fact, in itself, helped keep me going. Night after night I studied in the privacy of my room after finishing problem sets for my physics classes. I searched for provable errors or contradictions and found none. Paradoxes and passages I didn't fully understand, yes, but nothing that I could demonstrate with certainty as a contradiction or error. Instead, I found dozens of passages where the Bible accurately predicted future scientific discoveries and future historical events, some even thousands of years ahead of their time.

For example, I noticed that Genesis 1 matched the chronological order and the description of events in Earth's history,[1] and statements in Ecclesiastes, Jeremiah, and Romans described the unchanging nature of the laws of physics throughout the universe.[2] Daniel's prophecies of the rise and fall of future empires[3] and Ezekiel's prophecies concerning the second rebirth of Israel as a nation proved historically correct.[4] Such amazing and consistent predictive power, I deduced, could be explained only if the Bible authors, who spanned a considerable breadth of time, location, and culture, had been inspired by the One who brought the universe into existence.

I also noted that the Bible, unlike other books held sacred, described attributes of God and other truths that could not be explained within the length, width, height, and time dimensions we humans experience. These attributes and doctrines require the existence of either dimensions (or their equivalent) beyond the ones we experience or a God who exists and operates independent of our dimensions. Given that humans can visualize phenomena only in the dimensions they experience (despite mathematicians' ability to play with extra dimensions), the biblical references to these attributes and doctrines suggested that the Bible, unlike any other book, could not have sprung from mere human imagination, as spectacular as it may be.

This accumulation of observations and conclusions—that the Bible was free of historical and scientific error, could predict future events and discoveries, and described attributes of God that transcended human visualization capacity—seemed simultaneously thrilling and chilling. Although I still had unanswered questions, the personal implications of what I had discovered could not be ignored.

What if God's plans for me differed from the ones I had laid for myself? How would my parents and sisters, friends and strangers react to my new belief that I owed my life, my entire being, and future to God in gratitude for what Jesus Christ, the eternal Word, did for me through his sinless life, atoning sacrifice, and bodily resurrection? My life would no longer be my own to do with as I pleased. All this and more the Gideons had clarified for me in the back of that little free Bible. They also provided a place for me to sign and date, sealing the transfer of authority over my life.

Fear and pride held me back for a while. The anticipation of ridicule and rejection loomed large, not to mention awareness of my own weaknesses and deficits. For a few weeks I tried living like a Christian without actually *being* a Christian, as if it can be done. What a hollow experience that was! The more I tried to keep my thoughts and attitudes pure, the less I succeeded. Even my academic performance took a brief downturn, something I had not experienced since the start of grade two. Suddenly I recalled the story at the beginning of the book of Romans, describing how the rejection of truth leads to the darkening of the mind (Romans 1:21).

The moment of decision had come. I sat on my bed, perspiring and asking God to make me humble enough to surrender to him, but my tension only increased. Finally, it occurred to me that humbling myself was my part, and he would take me from there. An enormous wave of relief and peace rolled through me as I signed my name and recorded the details: August 7, 1964; 1:05 AM.

What if God's plans for me differed from the ones I had laid for myself?

No Random Timing

In terms of my preparation to give reasons for hope in Christ, the timing of my quest and eventual commitment seems strategic, not accidental. The challenge presented by King James English paled in comparison to other challenges—tests I would need to weather if ever God were to use me in helping others embrace faith and hope in Jesus Christ. At the University of British Columbia (UBC), I was in the midst of general education courses—philosophy, English, and French—all taught by atheistic professors. At the same time, I was involved in physics and astronomy societies where brilliant, aggressive proponents of atheism often spoke. Coincidentally, each argument or attack they raised just happened to meet with a viable response in what I had already read—or was about to read—in the Bible and in the scientific literature.

As I look back on my journey to faith, I recognize God's intricate orchestration of innumerable details, many more than my family's unexpected change of location, the help of an extraordinarily perceptive teacher and hardworking parents, access to great libraries, exposure to a certain biology textbook, saturation in the scientific method, a few words from a street preacher, extrication from church, a proverb from my father, the gift of a Gideon Bible, an overheard conversation, and a teacher's challenge. Often his working involved both Christians and non-Christians. Most had no idea God was using them in some supernatural way on my behalf. At least a few have become aware in the decades since.

My point in relating these stories is to affirm that the One who fine-tuned every aspect of the universe for our existence remains actively involved in the lives of the creatures he designed for relationship with him. For every encounter or event we recognize as divinely arranged, many more take place that we fail to recognize as such. According to Hebrews 13:2, many have entertained angels unaware. So, too, many have experienced spiritually significant encounters and events unaware.

My story also illustrates God's willingness and ways to provide light where and when it's needed. John writes in his first epistle that God's light encompasses his life, love, and truth. In the first chapter of his gospel account, John declares that God's light is available to every human being. Exactly how it comes, the text does not say, but God has many options. In the same chapter, John explains that each of us will be held accountable for our response to the light revealed to us. This accountability comes with a promise: whoever responds with openness to the light God has given will receive more light.

These words relieved the sense of responsibility I felt, that any believer may feel, for the response of the nonbelievers with whom we take the opportunity to share some spiritual truth. If they (or others within earshot) receive it and take it to heart, God guarantees to bring them additional life, love, and truth through other encounters and events in their life. God's promise of additional light must not be construed as a guarantee of their salvation. If a person chooses, at some point, to reject the light God has given, their capacity to receive more light becomes impaired. Nevertheless, we have cause to be optimistic. As Acts 2:21, 39 say (referring to Joel 2 with an emphasis on the paradoxical truth of human free will and divine sovereignty), "And everyone who calls on the name of the Lord will be saved.... The promise is for you and your children and for all who are far off—for all whom the Lord our God will call."

> **Whoever responds with openness to the light God has given will receive more light.**

Robert Dicke

The morning after signing my name in the back of my Gideon Bible, I awoke refreshed and rested, but everything around me looked the same as usual, and so did the face in my mirror. I could see that my signature was real, and I knew my commitment was real, but I wondered what changes I might see to make this new reality clearly evident. I also realized I would need more light, more understanding and evidence to share my faith with the highly skeptical people surrounding me. So much hinged on my confidence that the Bible is true from the first verse onward, but many astronomers and physicists still didn't share my certainty of a cosmic beginning.

As I began my sophomore year at UBC, I faced major frustration in trying to get my hands on the latest issues of the *Astronomical* and *Astrophysical Journals*. The university subscribed to just one copy of each, shared among hundreds of students and professors. How could I keep up with the research under such circumstances? Then, within days, I learned that as a physics major, if I could become a student member of the American Astronomical Society (AAS), I'd be eligible to purchase a subscription to both journals for only ten dollars a year! So, I quickly researched what it would take to become a member and learned that a current full member of the Society would have to recommend me and sign my application, vouching for my potential and intent to pursue a career in astronomy.

The then chairman of the physics department, George Volkoff, must be a member, I figured. After all, he and J. Robert Oppenheimer wrote a famous paper that predicted the existence of neutron stars. When I approached Dr. Volkoff about possibly recommending me, I learned to my amazement he was not a member. However, he told me he had just invited Robert Dicke, a distinguished AAS member, to come to UBC to address the physics department. Dr. Volkoff assured me that he and another professor familiar with my leadership role in the Royal Astronomical Society of Canada would urge Dicke to sign my application.

Several days later, I was called into Dr. Volkoff's office. My classmates teased me about being in some kind of trouble. Instead, as I entered the office, Robert Dicke was there to greet me. He asked about what aspects of astronomy I was currently studying, what kind of astronomy research I hoped to pursue in graduate school, and if I would be attending his lecture that afternoon. Apparently satisfied with my answers, he signed my application.

In his lecture, Dicke presented what was known as the Brans–Dicke cosmological model, which he boldly claimed would soon replace Einstein's theory of general relativity as well as big bang cosmological models. An ardent atheist, Dicke remained adamant that both general relativity and big bang cosmology *must* be wrong, given their implications concerning a cosmic beginning. Nevertheless, Dicke did mention possible observational outcomes that would invalidate his own model.

Within days of Dicke's signing my application, I received my first copy of the *Astrophysical Journal*. A few issues later, I noticed a paper by Dicke and two other authors alongside one by Arno Penzias and Robert Wilson, both articles discussing the meaning of excess cosmic radiation—now detectable thanks to an instrument designed by Dicke.

During World War II, Dicke had invented, assembled, and used a radiometer to set an upper limit on the cosmic background radiation: 20 Kelvin. In 1964, Peter Roll and David Wilkinson (two of Dicke's students and coauthors with Dicke and James Peebles) used a high-sensitivity Dicke radiometer and receiver to measure the radiation their mentor had determined would remain *if* the universe were actually expanding from an initial extremely hot state (a big bang). Dicke had calculated that the excess antenna temperature in that case would be between 3 and 5 Kelvin. Roll and Wilkinson had already begun making their measurements when Dicke received a phone call from Penzias and Wilson asking him to explain the mysterious excess radiation they had just found with the help of his radiometer, 3.5 Kelvin, ±1.0 Kelvin.

In 1978, Penzias and Wilson received the Nobel Prize in Physics for their discovery. Even though Dicke had designed the crucial instrument, predicted the significance of the excess radiation, and explained to Penzias and Wilson what they had discovered, he was overlooked, most likely because he refused to acknowledge the big bang creation event, the discovery his research and inventiveness had made possible.

I cannot overstate how these breakthrough discoveries, just months after my surrender to Christ, strengthened my faith. While I had become convinced of a cosmic creation event before, this new discovery removed any reasonable doubt about its existence, not in the virtually infinite past but only some 12–20 billion years ago. The universe had a beginning, just as the Bible had declared thousands of years ago. I felt a surge of confidence that I could defend my belief in the God of the Bible and in the Bible's message of God's redemptive plan to any of my fellow physics students.

First Encounter
My physics lab partner throughout my sophomore, junior, and senior years at UBC was an astute thinker and careful researcher named John Samson. John went on to become a geophysicist and for a number of years served as chair of the physics department at the University of Alberta. When I signed my name in the back of my Gideon Bible, John came to mind. I knew that my commitment

to being Christ's disciple meant telling others what I had done and encouraging them to do the same. Like me, they would need some assurance that Jesus Christ is, indeed, the Creator of everything, the Bible is true, and the good news it proclaims about God's purpose and plan to redeem us can be trusted. In other words, I was called to participate in some way in bringing people to Jesus Christ.

John was the first person I wanted to talk with about my newfound faith in Christ, but with him, the intimidation factor was high. I still struggled some with verbal fluency, and John made a habit of challenging everything I said until I could demonstrate to his satisfaction that it was true. With trepidation and yet a desire to let my friend in on my life-giving discovery, one afternoon after our last physics class of the day, I tried to get a spiritual conversation started.

The universe had a beginning, just as the Bible had declared thousands of years ago.

Before I could even put one sentence together, John stopped me. He said, "Hugh, I know you want to talk about something important to you. But, I really need to talk. I need to talk to someone about God. Do you know anyone on this campus who knows anything about God?"

For the next two hours John and I talked about God, the Bible, the Christian faith, and about how a few weeks earlier I had become a follower of Christ. John questioned me closely about how I became convinced that the Bible was supernaturally inspired and totally trustworthy. John was especially intent on testing the Bible's predictive power. When I told him that the second rebirth of Israel as a nation and subsequent developments in the modern nation of Israel precisely fulfilled biblical prophecy, John, true to form, said, "Prove it."

Two evenings later, we were both working in the main university library on three sets of exceptionally difficult physics problems. Strangely, an assignment we thought would take until two or three in the morning to complete we both finished at the same time, around midnight. With this extra time on our hands I asked John if he wanted to see the evidence he had asked for.

We went to the part of the library where microfilms of old newspapers were stored. We spent the next two hours comparing biblical prophecies about

Israel with newspaper stories about Israel published between 1945–1960 in the *Jerusalem Post, San Francisco Chronicle,* and *The Times* (London).

John saw with amazement how the newspaper reports affirmed the Bible's predictive accuracy. We spent other late-night sessions scanning the library's microfilms and talking about God and physics. Although John never made clear to me whether he repented and embraced God's offer of redemption in Christ, I observed that he no longer mocked Christians or Christianity. Years later, I met Christians who had been students of his at the University of Alberta. They told me John had encouraged their faith.

Proof of Concept

My encounter with John drove home to me the reliability of God's promise in Ephesians 2:10, not to mention the excitement of obeying 1 Peter 3:15–16. Initially I thought I had to be the one to set up spiritually significant encounters, but I saw that God had already prepared one for me. I thought I had to find a way to steer the conversation toward my reasons for hope in Jesus Christ, but as soon as I became prepared to offer them, God led me to someone who asked me for those reasons.

Does God intend for *all* of his disciples to experience encounters with people who need and want to know the reasons for our hope? Or does he choose a select few of his followers to endow with a special "gift" that enables them to be effective in bringing others to faith in Christ? The next chapter addresses these questions.

Chapter 6

Readiness and "the Gift"

Spiritual gifts, as a topic, rank high among church controversies of the past century or more. Respected pastors, teachers, theologians, psychologists, missionaries, and others draw diverse and conflicting interpretations from Paul's teaching about gifts in Romans 12, 1 Corinthians 12, and Ephesians 4. Some would say some or all the gifts ceased to be available after the birth of the church and the completion of the New Testament canon.[1] Others place major emphasis on the availability and expression of all the gifts, all the time.[2]

Rather than debate these conflicting views, I'd like to focus on what I see as Paul's main theme in all three of these and other gift-related passages: the Holy Spirit empowers every believer *to know God and to make him known*. Self-glorification or "special status" associated with gifts totally violates the purpose of the gifts, not to mention the character of Christ.

I like to point out that only one of these three lists of gifts includes a reference to evangelism, actually to "evangelist," and that's the Ephesians 4 list. There we read that in apportioning grace to each of his own, Christ gave us some apostles, prophets, evangelists, pastors, and teachers—for one clearly stated purpose: "to equip [God's] people for works of service, so that the body of Christ may be built up" (verse 12) in unity, in maturity, and in love, "as each part does its work" (verse 16). Notice the emphasis, here, rests on training.

Yes, some Christians certainly are uniquely effective as evangelists, but this passage makes clear they are given to the church as gifts to *equip* (train) God's people to serve in bringing others to Christ and to maturity in Christ. *All* Christ-followers play a part in calling others to him, according to Scripture. In 2 Corinthians 5, for example, we read that in reconciling us to himself through Christ, God gave each of us "the message of reconciliation" to pass along to others, letting them know that because of what Jesus accomplished, they can be reconciled to God, too, their sins no longer counting against them (verses

18–22).

I'm convinced God calls each of us to use whatever talents, skills, and gifts he endows us with to draw others toward him. To me, the differentiation of spiritual gifts implies that each Christian will "evangelize" (convey the good news to others) in a different but nonetheless productive way. In this context, every Christian is gifted for evangelism, but each Christian's manner of expressing that gift will be unique.

All **Christ-followers play a part in calling others to him.**

"Unique" also applies to the circumstances wherein we share the good news. In some places and situations, the barriers to the good news, the message of reconciliation, prove much stronger and higher than in others. Jesus and his disciples experienced this difference. The apostles and first missionaries certainly did, too. And yet, God provided supernatural power as needed, time and time again, to ensure his kingdom's ongoing advance.

Overcoming Hesitancy

When it comes to faith sharing, many of us hold back for any number of invalid reasons, and I've personally felt the pull of the big three: It's too scary, too hard, and too time-consuming. I would agree with all three *if not* for the availability of God's promised resources. God calls his followers to a challenging and arduous task, a work made more challenging and more arduous because of powerful opposition from "the world, the flesh, and the devil."[3] Only by full reliance upon the Holy Spirit can any Christian hope to participate in evangelism with effectiveness, and without becoming "weary and burdened." When even the weakest of us climbs into the yoke with Christ, we discover to our amazement that his work fits us well (which is what "easy" means, in this context) and the burden, while it doesn't evaporate, becomes "light" enough to manage.

I must add, however, that in sharing our faith we're touching upon something of utmost value, namely a human being's soul and spirit. The potential to cause harm can seem overwhelming. With my insensitivity to peoples' states of mind and emotion, the possibility that I might drive people farther away from Christ, rather than closer to him, gripped me, especially in the early days.

Perhaps you, too, have felt this fear of being offensive, or being wrong about someone's openness, or facing a question for which you have no good answer. The good news is that God can still use you. God *wants* to use you.

An Unlikely Evangelist

What does an effective evangelist look like? The picture that comes to many people's minds takes the shape of an effervescently friendly extrovert who can instantly make an emotional connection with anyone, anytime, anywhere; a persuasive person who can sell anything, including Jesus, to anyone; an articulate communicator with a ready wit and such personal warmth that others naturally want to be near.

In other words, the picture represents the opposite of me in every way. As someone with characteristics of autism spectrum disorder, I struggle mightily to read social and emotional cues, even my own emotions. When it comes to reading body language, facial expression, and tone of voice, I am virtually illiterate. Given that most communication between people is nonverbal, you could say I'm severely handicapped.

As a high school sophomore, I was one of twenty-five students selected to be part of an amazing program called the Joe Berg Science Seminars. A battery of written tests determined who'd be chosen.

A year into the program, a research psychologist conducted one-on-one assessments of each of us. Let's just say I baffled the woman. I could not put cartoon panels depicting relationship interactions in the correct chronological order. Even when she gave me hints about the relationships pictured, I could not discern a sequence. My every attempt failed.

The University of British Columbia also required incoming freshmen to take a battery of various aptitude tests, followed up by an appointment with a psychologist. After reviewing these test scores and observing my mannerisms, including my lack of eye contact with him, he said, "Hugh, you'll be a success at whatever academic or career path you choose, as long as it does not involve interaction with people." He encouraged me to find a research position that allowed me to study and work alone.

A year later, when I came to faith in Christ, I knew that becoming his disciple meant a commitment, in spite of my communication handicaps, to declaring my faith, and the reasons for my faith, with people not yet aware of who he is or of the gift he offers. I saw evangelism not as an option but rather as a command from God to every believer.

This command presented a problem for me. How would I even recognize an opportunity to share my newly confirmed beliefs with my fellow physics students? How would I start the conversation or detect if someone were remotely interested in what I had to say?

I only knew that I needed to keep on studying to gain a better grasp of God's Word. Then, in the midst of studying again the Old Testament prophets, God stunned me with an obvious opportunity to share my faith. As I described in the previous chapter, my physics lab partner suddenly asked me if I knew anything about God. I told him I was currently reading the book of Ezekiel, and he wanted to know what I was learning.

In other words, God provided an opportunity in spite of my communication handicaps. He has continued to do so in the years that followed.

Cracked Clay Jars

Over time, I've come to see my handicaps as tools God not only *could* but *would* use for his purposes. My inability to read body language and emotional cues has surprisingly proved beneficial on several occasions. God's plan for me doesn't necessarily require superb relational skills. He is the ultimate relater. And I learned I could count on him to bring others alongside me, not only to compensate for my deficiencies but also to help me learn and grow in those very areas. To put it another way, my weaknesses have not impaired my usefulness to God. He wants me to let *his* strengths, *his* power and glory, to shine out from me—and to make me a team player.

After all, God blesses every human being with weaknesses and "handicaps," as well as strengths and capabilities. These differ from person to person, but we all have them.

It seems our shortcomings do more than our strengths to encourage reliance upon God rather than upon ourselves. When we share our faith, our weaknesses may help those we share with to direct their attention to God, rather than to us.

One passage that removed a huge load of stress as I made my first fumbling attempts to spreading the good news—and still keeps it at bay—is 2 Corinthians 4:6–7. The apostle Paul here explains that the same God who calls forth light to dispel darkness (as in Genesis 1:3) now makes his light shine in and from our hearts, visible to all who are willing to see it. "But we have this treasure" he says, "in jars of clay to show that this all-surpassing power [God's glory as revealed in Christ] is from God and not from us."

In other words, our attempts to patch up, hide, or cover over the cracks in our jars diminishes the release of light from God's glory within. By allowing

God's light to shine through our acknowledged weaknesses and limitations, we allow nonbelievers to recognize the power and glory radiating from us as God's, not something we could possibly manufacture. Paul drives home his point in the account of his struggle with a painful difficulty, or "thorn" in his flesh. God assures him, "My grace is sufficient for you, for my power is made perfect in weakness" (2 Corinthians 12:9).

> **Our weaknesses may help those we share with to direct their attention to God, rather than to us.**

Humans, Not Angels

One day early on in my evangelistic efforts, another stress reliever occurred to me: Humans are not the only intelligent spiritual creatures God made. He also made angels.

Angels wield more power than human beings, and the righteous angels are without sin. They have access to both heavenly and earthly knowledge. They can appear to any human being anytime, anywhere, and in any form. Any one of God's angels can offer a perfect presentation of the Christian message. What's more, people seem much more likely to pay attention to an angel than to a fellow human being.

Did God choose to use human messengers because of a shortage of angelic messengers? According to Revelation 5:11, the number of angels exceeds the highest number used in first century Greek literature: myriads of myriads, or hundreds of millions. No shortage, there.

With such assets at his disposal, it seems odd that God would choose mere humans, with all our inadequacies and ineptness, especially mine. Only after several years of sharing my faith did the reason become clear to me. When I did come to the realization, I felt chagrined that it took me so long to grasp.

In his letter to Philemon, a leader (as well as host) of the house church in Colossae, Paul writes, ". . . I pray that the sharing of your faith may become effective for the full knowledge of every good thing that is in us for the sake of Christ" (ESV). Do you see what Paul's prayer implies? An invaluable personal benefit derives from active involvement in spreading the good news. The sharing of our faith brings more than a potentially life-changing opportunity for the person we share with. It enhances, or "fills up," our grasp of "every good thing" available to us in Christ. According to Paul, then, one key to gaining the kind of understanding that leads to more faith, hope, love, joy, peace, patience, kindness, goodness, faithfulness, gentleness, and self-control comes from sharing with others what we already possess.

Through observation and experience, I've learned that participation in making Christ known ("evangelism") really is a gift—to me and to everyone who actively engages in it. Every aspect of it, from preparing our hearts and minds to actually communicating with others, builds in us more of the mind and character of our Lord Jesus Christ (Romans 12:1–2).

Chapter 7

Ready for Change

During my last two years at the University of British Columbia and my five and a half years at the University of Toronto, my research studies in astronomy and physics absorbed so much time and energy that I rarely had a conversation about anything else. I do recall trying to find a group of people who shared my convictions about God's revelation in Scripture and in nature. Frankly, without knowing any Christians, I wasn't sure where to start. Obviously, my search predated Google.

Despite some wariness about churches due to my parents' experience, I remember scanning the religion section of the *Toronto Star* several times for a promising ad, something near the campus if possible, given that my modes of transportation included two feet and, weather permitting, a bicycle. (Not until years after leaving Toronto did I learn of Peoples Church, thirteen miles north of the University.) The few churches I checked out rejected either the trustworthiness of nature's record or the inspiration and accuracy of the Bible. Others turned out to be cults. Soon I quit looking and turned my full attention to completing my study of quasars (quasi-stellar objects in the far reaches of space) and distant galaxies. Occasionally I made an effort to open conversation about faith within my small research cohort, but my efforts fell flat, as far as I could tell.

As I was finishing up my PhD, I applied for a postdoctoral position at the California Institute of Technology (Caltech) and was thrilled to be accepted. I must admit that the proximity of Caltech's radio telescopes to the Sierra Nevada mountain range had a little something to do with my excitement. God had everything to do with it!

High Alpine Dinner
The hallways, offices, and libraries of Caltech's Robinson Laboratory (a

building dedicated to astronomy teaching and research) offered a surprising (to me) number of opportunities to share my faith. I noted, however, that conversations with my research colleagues proved much more engaging and impactful when they took place in a beautiful natural setting.

Caltech's radio observatory in California's Owens Valley sits less than an hour's drive from several spectacular mountain trails, including access to stunningly beautiful parts of Kings Canyon National Park. After one observing run, I invited a visiting astronomer (twenty years older than I) and an astronomy undergrad (eight years younger than I) to hike with me into a high alpine meadow where we could camp.

After dinner, we gazed across a lake at towering peaks and waterfalls. I asked my two companions what they thought of the view. They both declared it "gorgeous beyond words or photos to describe." Then two more questions occurred to me: "How do you feel when you look upon such a scene?" and "How do you explain the beauty of this place?"

One of my companions, a self-identified atheist, described feelings of euphoria, contentment, and deep peace. The other said he was having a weird, almost scary, but at the same time calming spiritual experience. Later I learned he came from a nonpracticing Jewish family. These questions led to a nearly two-hour discussion about creation, God, and God's possible purposes for the universe, Earth, and human beings. From that time forward, our conversations about Jesus Christ, the Bible, and God's plans for humanity flowed comfortably, frequently, and in-depth.

Bugaboos Blizzard

About a year later, the same two companions accompanied me on a mountaineering vacation to the Bugaboos in British Columbia. On the first day, we packed all our gear to the Conrad Kain Hut, a three-story structure shared with about forty other climbers, including one we had met on a trail in California. On the second day, the three of us ascended to within a few feet of the summit of Eastpost Spire. Elated, we headed back to the hut, a light snow just beginning to fall. That night, the light snowfall turned into a full-on blizzard.

A three-day blizzard during the first week of August stunned everyone in the hut. As you can imagine, it did not take long for cabin fever to set in. Though disappointed at being grounded, I had come prepared. The blizzard gave me time to do an in-depth study of the book of Revelation along with the Old Testament books it repeatedly references.

On day two of the blizzard, some of the climbers became curious about what I was studying so intently, and why. Their query led to a six-hour discussion involving more than twenty of the climbers. Topics ranged from scientific evidence for God's existence, to God's reasons for creating the universe with its particular laws of physics and dimensions, to why God created human beings, to how Israel came together as a nation for a second time in history, to other aspects of biblical prophecy, to whether or when Jesus Christ would return to Earth.

To my amazement and joy, none disputed my conclusion that Jesus Christ was God and that he may well be returning to Earth. Some wanted to know more about how to establish an eternal relationship with him. Many more simply wanted me to provide an estimated date for Christ's return to Earth. Sadly, I learned why. They admitted to wanting to know so they'd have an idea when to elevate their climbing ventures to death-defying levels. They'd rather die climbing an impossibly difficult rock wall, they said, than submit their lives to the Creator and Savior.

The blizzard that kept us all inside the Conrad Kain Hut for three days taught me that every human being worships something. Many of my scientist peers worship the thrill of scientific discoveries. Many climbers like those I met in the hut worship the thrill of climbing sheer rock faces. In other words, addiction comes in many forms, and addicts feel no apparent concern for the emptiness their addiction leads to or for the ultimate hope, purpose, and destiny it keeps them from experiencing.

Being prepared for spiritual conversation is a thrill like none other.

The blizzard taught me something else, too. Being prepared for spiritual conversation is a thrill like none other. Even if many or most reject our words, at least a few may respond—if not right away, then perhaps sometime down the road. That possibility alone brings incomparable joy.

Ian Lockhart

When I arrived at Caltech, I was given the front part of an office that had been partitioned into two. An Australian astronomer, Ian Lockhart, who had arrived for his postdoctoral research six months earlier, now had to pass through my office to get to his. I had doubts about whether he'd appreciate sharing this office space, but we both felt glad for the opportunity to work at Caltech.

Almost immediately Ian spotted the Bible on my desk. He asked, "Are you one of those Bible-thumping Christians?" I acknowledged being a Christian but added that I couldn't recall ever thumping a Bible or thumping anyone else with it.

Ian, who announced himself as an atheist, then surprised me by asking if I'd mind answering questions, once in a while, about Christianity and the Bible. "Once in a while" turned out to mean "daily."

Every day, Ian quizzed me about the Bible or some aspect of the Christian faith. Without fail, a couple of hours later, he would go downstairs to the coffee room and repeat selected parts of whatever I had told him to the other astronomers gathered there. Because my office sat right above the coffee room, I could hear Ian's mimicry of my words and the laughter it always drew from his audience.

I decided not to let the mockery stop me from answering Ian's so-called "questions," despite the pain of his ridicule. I reasoned that at least a few of the seeds of truth I was scattering might take root in the heart of at least one of those astronomers—perhaps even in Ian—if the Holy Spirit planted it there.

After about six months, Ian told me he could no longer consider himself an atheist. My hopes rose for a moment until he announced he had become a Zen Buddhist. When asked why, he replied, "No other religion offers salvation, or at least peace, at such a low price."

About four months later, Ian announced another change. He said that although the price for Zen Buddhism seemed a bargain, the salvation it promised delivered no real peace. During this conversation he conceded that Christianity offered "the goods," but at a price that to him still seemed way too high. Ian placed a high value on independence.

For the next two months, our conversations revolved around Ian's effort to bargain down the cost of salvation through Jesus Christ. Meanwhile, although the coffee room hilarity continued, Ian's tone changed. His mocking tone evolved from derisive to good-natured. Ian began to show me respect, and his questions became more serious, more deeply probing.

One day Ian walked into the astronomy group's coffee room at Caltech and told everyone present, "I can no longer ridicule what Hugh Ross tells me about the Bible or Christianity because last night I submitted my life to Jesus Christ." Ian's statement brought stunned silence to the room. For the next twenty minutes, the only sound emanating from that room was a faint slurping.

Ian was thirty-two years old when he gave his life to Christ. Just ten months later, this robust appearing young man suffered a massive heart attack and died. What a shock to the Caltech community! What a grief to me! As you may imagine, his sudden death had a sobering effect on our fellow astronomers, and it led to multiple opportunities for discussion about priorities, relationships, and preparation for what comes next. In retrospect, I see that the experience of knowing and sharing my faith with Ian prepared me more effectively than any evangelism training class or program available. He had challenged me on nearly every point and every question I'd ever hear from a skeptical mind. The Holy Spirit used him to prepare me for my future as much as he used me to prepare Ian for his.

Sensing an Opportunity

Christians often ask me how we can know if someone is prepared by God to hear reasons to believe. My response: never assume they're not. Once a conversation begins, often with a question, the Holy Spirit guides. After all, he is the one who draws people to Christ. However, he calls upon us to take some initiative. Developing sensitivity to his guidance takes a combination of prayer and practice.

Prayer helps us maintain a gentle, respectful demeanor even when someone's response seems rude or dismissive.

We can anticipate occasions to interact with people or times when we will be walking, standing, or sitting beside strangers. In that anticipation, we can pray that the Holy Spirit will lead us into spiritually productive conversations, no matter how brief the interaction. Prayer helps us maintain a gentle, respectful demeanor even when someone's response seems rude or dismissive. Through trial and error, we discover what kinds of questions spark conversations with the different people we're likely to encounter. Through trial and error, we also discover ways to improve our readiness.

Ready to Fail and Grow

When the Christian clubs on the Caltech campus heard about my personal outreach among research colleagues, they invited me to speak at an outreach event they would organize. I agreed to present "Scientific Evidence for the Christian Faith and the Reliability of the Bible." Given the outcome of my interactions with Ian Lockhart, I went into the event feeling fairly confident.

In all honesty, that event did not go well. My words seemed to fall flat, and during the question-and-answer session, atheist graduate students and postdocs disputed several of the points I had tried to make in my talk, but they weren't giving me specifics. My attempts to answer their objections did not seem to satisfy them, either.

Rather than just walk away disappointed after the event was over, as I felt like doing, I stayed and asked those who had most vocally reacted to my message and my answers to help me out. First, I asked if they would point out where they saw weaknesses in my case for the trustworthiness of the Bible and the Christian message. Second, I asked if they could point out anything in my delivery, including my mannerisms or my tone of voice, that interfered with their willingness to accept what I had presented.

They said "yes" to both questions and eagerly offered their feedback. For the next ninety minutes, they explained where my approach or explanations had been less than effective while I took detailed notes, both written and mental. For the next two months, I used those notes to research and develop a stronger, clearer case and to improve my speaking skills, including my demeanor.

I'm still working to improve both the reasons I present and the way I present them. That event was not the last one in which my weaknesses were on display. However, I can say all events and encounters with skeptics and atheists since then have been considerably less embarrassing.

That painful evening I learned a valuable lesson. If the reasons we offer for our hope in Jesus Christ do not go over well, we have an opportunity to find out why. The people we engage with our reasons may serve as our best resource for improving our message, if we will humbly listen and, with God's gracious help, refrain from getting defensive.

Dave Rogstad

Not long after I moved into my office and began the running dialogue with Ian, I met a Christian who made a world of difference in my life. As I have said, when I arrived at Caltech to begin my postdoctoral research, I had been a Christian for eight and a half years without really getting to know well another serious Christian. During those years, I had fleeting encounters with people who may have been believers, and one who was a believer but a distracted one, but not someone who could encourage my growth in Christ.

Part of my difficulty was the intensity of my research. It required an exhausting level of focus, for all but the last two to three months, as my 700-page dissertation was being finalized, printed, and reviewed. During those months, a strong desire to find and spend time with fellow Christians and to be spiritually challenged grew within me.

Even though I had virtually given up on church, I wanted to be involved in some kind of Christian ministry. But what and with whom? As it turned out, the same Bible and Christian books that had caught Ian's attention eventually caught the eye of another scholar, a researcher from a different group. Dave Rogstad had just returned from postdoctoral studies in Holland to take up a position as senior research fellow in radio astronomy.

When Dave saw the Bible and books, he stepped into my office to ask if I was a Christian. I answered, "Yes." Dave looked

If the reasons we offer for our hope in Jesus Christ do not go over well, we have an opportunity to find out why.

skeptical. He wanted to know if I was a *real* Christian, one who actually believed and studied the Bible and openly talked about it with others. I nodded and told him about my conversations with other Caltech astronomers and, in particular, my office partner.

Just as my scruffy appearance and rough edges raised questions for Dave, so did his clean-cut appearance and special vocabulary in speaking about the Bible and Christianity concern me. He bore more than a slight resemblance to the zealous cultists I'd encountered in Toronto.

Our mutual concerns evaporated during a long car ride to the Owens Valley Radio Observatory. He learned about my secular background, and I learned about his Christian family heritage. Dave showed me what a mature Christian looked like, and the view inspired me to do some catching up. Recognizing my uneasiness about church, Dave invited me to join him at a Christian conference on building Christlike character, and I eagerly agreed to go.

What a spiritual breakthrough that event was for me! For the first time in my life, I found myself surrounded by Christians, a few thousand of them at once, committed to deepening their relationship with Christ and widening their spiritual influence. I felt something I had no words to describe—a sense of unity and belonging and joy that wells up in worship to God. Until I experienced it, I didn't even realize what I had been longing for since the beginning of my walk with Christ.

After the conference, Dave launched a home study where about fifteen of us reviewed the hundreds of Scripture passages cited during the conference. Together we endeavored to put into practice what we were learning and to hold each other accountable. One evening after the study, Dave presented me with a challenge. He asked me to consider going beyond the Caltech campus and my colleagues there to share my reasons for believing the Bible is true and for putting my faith in Jesus Christ. He seemed to think nonscientists would respond even more positively and enthusiastically than my research peers to the scientific evidences I had accumulated for the Christian faith.

I recall asking Dave, "Where am I going to meet these nonscientists?" Dave replied, "Across the street from the Caltech campus!"

He meant metaphorically, but I took him literally, as someone on the spectrum would. I really did walk across the street from the campus, and to my amazement, in talking to people along that street, I discovered what Dave had said was true. Nonscientists proved more receptive to my science- and history-based reasons for faith in Christ than I could have imagined.

Soon thereafter Dave introduced me to a truck driver and his wife, who had, just days ago, committed their lives to Jesus Christ. After hearing the story of how I became a Christian, this couple peppered me with questions about the Bible, science, history, and what it means to live the Christian life. They asked if I would be willing to answer questions for their relatives and friends. God used dinners at this couple's house to bring many of their relatives and friends to Christ. Within weeks, I found myself teaching home Bible studies to packed houses every Tuesday and Saturday evening. Before long, I recruited Dave to help me lead one of the Bible studies that formed around those who were coming to Christ.

Dave let me know the time had come for me to get involved in a church. He gave me a list of six great churches within easy bike-riding distance from Caltech. One of the six was the church Dave and his family attended. After checking out all six, I settled on Dave's church and discovered that he had already spoken to the leaders there about my outreach activities. As soon as I began attending, they encouraged me to continue these activities *and* offered their support.

By this time, I had experienced the depth of joy and fulfillment that comes with seeing people respond to evidence for the truth of God's Word by choosing to follow Jesus Christ. As much as I delighted in stretching the frontiers of knowledge about quasars and galaxies, this evangelistic work held eternal significance. That's more than I could say for the work I had spent most of my life to this point preparing for—or thinking I was preparing for. Perhaps God was preparing me for a change of direction.

Nonscientists proved more receptive to my science- and history-based reasons for faith in Christ.

Immigration and Naturalization Service Employees

Leaders at the church Dave and I attended during my years as a research fellow at Caltech had no idea that my visa was expiring and I would be leaving soon for Europe or back to Canada to continue my research. When Dave told them, they asked, "Do you think there's a way we can keep him here?" Dave knew I would need a different kind of visa, and an inquiry began.

According to the US Immigration and Naturalization Service (INS, now known as the US Citizenship and Immigration Services), I could apply for an H-1B work visa *if*

1. the church could demonstrate the need for a specialized staff position,
2. no known US citizen with the qualifications to fill that position wanted it, and
3. I could demonstrate my qualifications to fill it.

The church leaders said they were willing to give it a try if I was. So we all did our part and left the outcome to God.

Given the church's proximity to Caltech, the Jet Propulsion Laboratory, Fuller Seminary, and multiple engineering and technology firms, the church could honestly make a case for their need of an outreach pastor who possessed a PhD in science, an advanced degree (or equivalent) in theology, alignment with the church's doctrinal statement, and proven effectiveness in evangelism.

The INS accepted the church's case for the newly created position, but they wanted "proof" that I met all the stated qualifications. The science degree was already in hand, a Fuller faculty member rigorously tested me and wrote a statement vouching for my qualifications in theology, the pastors affirmed my commitment to the church's doctrinal statement, and I prepared a packet of the topical papers, outreach surveys, and Bible study lessons I had produced in the course of my volunteer activities. That's the bundle of materials we sent off to the INS.

Six weeks later I received a call from the INS agent responsible for approving my visa application. He asked, "What did you put in the package you sent?" I gave him a quick overview and asked if he needed something more.

"I don't think so," he said, "other than an explanation for what happened to the staff person I assigned to review it." He went on to say that this woman had spent several hours going over the materials rather than the expected 20 to 30 minutes, even taking them home with her for several consecutive evenings. And, what seemed even stranger, she had returned to work with a significantly altered demeanor or disposition, from short-tempered and irritable to the exact opposite.

Instead of trying to explain, I encouraged him to ask her. Soon thereafter, my H-1B visa arrived in the mail, and I had a new title, Minister of Evangelism. Meanwhile, I began handing off my research projects to others at Caltech, but I retained my regular reading of the scientific journals, even adding a few more to broaden my awareness of new developments not only in cosmology and astronomy but also in other disciplines. These provided, and still do, an endless and growing stream of evidences for the Creator's fine-tuning of the universe, Earth, and life toward fulfillment of his redemptive plan.

Loaded Gun

My new role as a member of the church's pastoral team took me into unfamiliar territory, but at every turn I sensed that God would use one aspect or another of my past experience and even my personal deficits to prepare me and equip me. My lack of sensitivity to my environment, both physical and emotional, proved especially helpful, at times. But I also had some very big lessons still to learn, especially about ministering solo, as I had been used to.

One evening a new believer in one of my Bible study groups asked me if I'd please pay a visit to a friend of his. This friend had big struggles, he said, and needed to hear about Jesus from someone mature enough to gain his respect and answer his questions. I agreed, on one condition.

"Is your friend *willing* to have me come?" I asked.

"I'll check," he replied.

The next week at study this man assured me his friend wanted me to come, and he urged me to go soon because the man's troubles seemed to be worsening. I would have been wise to ask more questions, but in my eagerness to help, I went, and I knocked.

The door flew open, bringing me face-to-face with the barrel of a (presumably) loaded revolver. The face of the man holding it roiled with emotion. Oddly, a wave of peace and calm, rather than terror, washed over me. An inner voice assured me no one would be harmed and showed me a man in desperate need of someone to listen and point him gently to the only One who could heal the wounds in his soul.

Observing my calm demeanor, the man relaxed, slightly. He growled, "You're not the police, are you?" Immediately I identified myself as his friend's Bible study leader. With a quick look past me to the right and left, he waved me inside with his gun. His wife and small children huddled, shaking, in a corner of the room.

The man and I sat across his family's kitchen table from each other, the gun still in his hand as he poured out his tale of woe. He had lost his job, felt like a failure, suffered harassment from his neighbors, and hated everyone in authority, especially the police. Nodding in the direction of his wife and little ones, he muttered, "They're the only reason not to use this gun on myself."

The man clearly had endured mistreatment and misunderstanding by many people in his life, and I acknowledged his deep pain. Cautiously I mentioned how the deep resentment he carried toward those people seemed to be extending their damage and hurting his family even more. When I dared to bring up the healing power of forgiveness, he sighed deeply. He acknowledged what I said as true but declared it "utterly impossible." He said, "There's no way I can forgive. I don't have it in me."

To his surprise, I agreed. After a moment's pause, I explained that the desire and capacity to forgive can come only from the Creator of the universe, the Creator-Forgiver-Restorer, Jesus Christ. "He can and will provide, if asked," I assured him. The man's wife now pleaded with him to listen to me.

The man looked up and said, "I guess the first step is to put this thing down." He laid the gun on the table. We continued to talk and, in the end, prayed together. I learned that before I arrived, the neighbors had heard him yelling and threatened to call the police and have him arrested. All the more agitated, he loaded the revolver and promised to unload it into the first cop to show up at his door. In an attempt to lighten the mood, we agreed it's a good thing I looked too scrawny to be in law enforcement.

Within days, the man turned in his gun at the local police station. He did not let go of all his hurts or give his life to Christ right away. That process took a few years. However, that evening marked the beginning of his spiritual journey. He had heard God's voice that night, and so had I. From that time on, I took someone with me on all outreach calls.

A Hospital Visit

Another man in one of my Bible studies asked me to make a "chaplain" call. An old buddy of his lay in the burn ward at a local, understaffed medical center. I asked him to go with me, but he said, "I can't," hinting at reasons he did not wish to disclose. Overhearing our conversation, three other men in our study, all new believers, bravely agreed to accompany me—and I'm grateful they did.

The ward resembled nothing I had ever seen, except perhaps in a movie. The cavernous rectangle with closely packed patient beds lining all walls appeared utterly devoid of medical staff. It took us awhile to find the man we had hoped to visit, and when we did he called out gruffly, "Leave me alone!"

We turned to exit, eager to escape the awful sights and smells but suddenly realized we could make ourselves useful by helping to clean up some of the mess—scattered trash, urine puddles, and more. As we busied ourselves, one of the patients commented, "You guys must be *real* Christians. Will you stay and talk with us? We never get visitors."

Many of these men, we learned, came from the most notorious neighborhoods in Los Angeles. Nearly all had been to church at some point during childhood, but they had little to no clue about who Jesus was or why he had come or what he taught. They wanted to know.

So, the four of us split up to talk with as many patients as we could, one or two at a time. After an hour or more had gone by, two young interns poked their heads through the door. Perhaps they assumed we were cultists sent to brainwash their patients because they abruptly asked us to get out. At that moment the patients rose to our defense.

"You don't understand," they said. "These guys were about to leave but we *asked* them to stay. They're answering our questions, and we still have more!" The interns shrugged and said we could stay for a few more minutes.

During the next half hour, the patients called out one question after another. As we left, we gave them our Bibles and I pulled a few papers from my bag that addressed some of their questions in more depth. They thanked us profusely, and the four of us returned to our car, amazed, exhausted, and elated all at the same time. That day God gave us an opportunity to *live* what we had been reading about serving others and doing what God had prepared in advance for us to do (Ephesians 2:10, again).

Adult Bookstore

These Bible study participants learned important lessons about prayer, too, when an adult bookstore opened up a few blocks from where we met, near the center of the famous Rose Parade route. Along with the store came the usual cast of characters and temptations, none of them good for the health of our community. Not knowing exactly what the Lord wanted us to do about it, I invited the group to join me for a day of prayer and fasting.

About fifteen friends gathered in my apartment that day, seeking direction and asking God to protect the men, women, and children of our city, as well as those who pass through. As we continued, our prayers became much more specific about how we might partner with God in dealing with this situation.

By the end of the day, we had come to agreement on our next steps. We would gather again for prayer, this time recruiting more Christians to join us. Then small groups of us would take turns the following Saturday, praying all day on the sidewalk in front of the place. Then, after one more day of prayer and fasting, we would commission some of the women in our group to speak with the women hanging around the bookstore and some of the men to speak with the men, inviting them to discover the lasting love and fulfillment available only through Jesus.

As we put some details to the plan that took shape through our prayers, more than a few of our group expressed hesitancy. The plan seemed extraordinarily bold, if not aggressive. However, during the last hour of that first prayer day, everyone came together in agreement and committed to taking whatever role God called them to. We readied ourselves to take a step outside our comfort zone.

We did gather for additional days of prayer and fasting together, but not for our outreach to the adult bookstore. The need evaporated. Within a week of our first prayer day, the owners packed up and moved out. Another tenant of a totally different kind was now preparing to move in. As you can imagine, a sense of awe and wonder came over us. It seemed clear that God had intervened, as soon as, maybe even *before* we stepped up to pray and fast together in seeking God's leading in dealing with the adult bookstore's challenge to our community's morality. Life seemed more exciting every day now.

Looking back on those early years of my relationship with Dave, I believe no other human being could have persuaded me, prepared me, and opened a door for me to leave astronomy research for a career in ministry. That our paths intersected where they did, when they did, and how they did, seems beyond random. Our meeting and friendship impacted both of us in profound ways.

Dave says something happened in his life, as well as mine, as a result of our relationship. Before I showed up at Caltech, Dave had met with frustration in his efforts to share the good news of Christ with his colleagues. Presenting them with what's called "the moral argument" for God (awareness of absolute good and evil depends on the reality of God's existence) seemed to fall flat. But, he noticed, some did respond positively to my scientific evidences for the God of the Bible. So, Dave changed his approach and began to stir up interest. This led to some fruitful encounters and increased his joy. He went on to become a leader and teacher at our church, even helping to plant a new church that sprang from our mutual outreach ministries. Dave still works alongside me to challenge and encourage me.

> **We readied ourselves to take a step outside our comfort zone.**

Atheist Club President

Through the years since transitioning to ministry, I have spoken in dozens of public schools, thanks to my unusual combination of credentials, and I always appreciate those opportunities. Not long after joining the pastoral staff, one of the students in the church youth group asked me to speak in her English class at a nearby public high school. The class had been studying a work by Mark Twain in which Twain poked fun at belief in God and mockingly argued for atheism.

Emboldened by Twain's words, and the teacher's willingness to discuss the topic, some of the atheist students in the class raised their own objections to belief in God, especially the Christian God. Many of their objections had to do with science, which led the Christian students in the class, including the one from my church, to ask if they could invite a scientist who believed in God to respond.

The request went all the way up the chain to the district superintendent, who saw my curriculum vitae and approved. The teacher allowed me to spend half of the class time summarizing what I considered the best scientific reasons for belief in God. The rest of the time could be used for questions and discussion.

As hands began to shoot up around the room, one student blurted, "It's true! It's all true!" After a moment of stunned silence, he continued, "What can I do to avoid judgment?" I looked at the teacher, who let me know with a nod that I had the freedom to answer this question. The whole class listened attentively as I explained God's offer of redemption and how to receive it. He thanked me and bowed his head. Not until after class ended that day did I learn why the rest of the class seemed so wide-eyed.

This young man had presided over the campus Atheist Club. A new election would have to be scheduled, but the number of candidates dwindled as he shared his change of mind and heart with other students, including fellow club officers. Some of them followed his lead and came to Christ.

Kathy Drake

Without knowing it at the time, Dave paved the way for yet another dramatic change in my life. Dave and his wife knew a young woman, the daughter of family friends at the church they had formerly attended. She had attended Dave's wedding with her parents, but after Dave left for a research stint in Holland, they lost contact. When Dave returned to Southern California a few years later, he and his wife and children became involved in a different church.

Kathy and her parents rarely missed a Sunday at church, but one weekend Kathy's mom was feeling too weak from a recent surgery to engage in all her usual social interactions there, including choir and Sunday class. So, she and Kathy decided this might be a good time to visit a different church, one they'd heard good things about. After being seated way off to one side, where they could barely see the pulpit, they began to have doubts about their decision, but to leave in the middle of service seemed inappropriate.

At one point in the service the worship leader invited people to stand and greet those around them. The first faces to turn in Kathy and her mom's direction in this crowded sanctuary belonged to none other than Dave and his wife, Diane. After a moment of stunned amazement, they greeted and hugged and agreed to talk after service.

During this happy reunion, Dave asked Kathy about her personal and professional life. She told him she had completed her master's degree, was working in a job she enjoyed at the University of Southern California, but was struggling to find Christian fellowship. Dave suggested a Bible study he knew of, but Kathy resisted. "I'm not looking for a singles social club, Dave," she said. "I've been to more than enough of those." As they parted, they exchanged phone numbers and commented again on the "crazy coincidence" of the morning.

The next afternoon, Kathy got a phone call from Dave with the address and other details about the study he had recommended. He ended with the comment, "They're meeting tonight, and I told them you'd be coming."

Irritated by Dave's presumptuousness, she told her parents, "I'm not going!" But, at the last moment, she felt a tug she could not seem to resist. So off she went, not knowing what to expect. Once there, she felt certain that a divine hand had coordinated the bizarre events of the past two days. She met people her age, a few married and others not yet, serious about studying God's Word and participating in God's work to benefit their community and the wider world.

Nine months later, Dave told me about this same Bible study. He described it as a group of strong believers, eager to grow and advance Christ's kingdom but nearly all from Christian homes and well-churched since childhood. He said, "They want to share their faith with non-Christians, but they just don't know how." Would I go there, he asked, to help them learn how to reach non-Christians?

Like Kathy, I protested. After all, I was already leading two Bible studies. I didn't have time for a third. The next day, Dave dropped by my office at Caltech to tell me he had contacted the host about my coming. All I could do was shake my head.

Reluctantly, I showed up on my bike and parked it between a couple of the sports cars in front of the house. *What had I gotten myself into?* No doubt they wondered the same when I entered, looking like the stereotypical mad scientist—complete with wild hair, muttonchops, and an outfit purchased almost entirely from my local supermarket. At the time I had no awareness what prompted the raised eyebrows and elbow nudges, but now I get it.

I didn't meet Kathy the first time I attended this Bible study. Apparently, she had taken a trip. I certainly do remember her first week back with the group. She approached me after the teaching time to ask if I was a scientist. How could she have guessed? When I said yes, she asked me how I found a way to accept both the scientific story and the biblical story of origins. Later she told me what had prompted her question. Her older brother, whom she dearly loves, had walked away from trust in the Bible and from Christianity altogether based on what he perceived as an obvious contradiction between Genesis 1 and nature's record.

Kathy expressed astonishment to hear that long before I got to know Christians, nature's record caused me to trust the Bible, including Genesis 1. My first reading of that passage had convinced me that the Bible demanded further investigation. Eventually I concluded that the Bible must be the Word of God, accurate in every way, including its interface with science and history.

That evening's conversation became just the first of many. Of all the Bible study participants I had met, Kathy showed the strongest desire to become equipped for outreach to nonbelievers, especially those with little to no church background. She also recognized my passion for reaching and teaching and privately asked God to help her help me. She had noticed some of my many communications challenges—my tendency to either stare or avoid eye contact, stand stiffly, recoil from touch, and use formal language.

At the time, neither of us knew anything about autism spectrum disorders. Not knowing probably worked to our benefit. It made me work harder to implement Kathy's gentle recommendations. It led Kathy to chalk up my peculiarities to my saturation in not one but two foreign cultures: Canadian and Caltech-ian.

Rather than criticizing my appearance, she explained that my wardrobe choices and personal grooming sometimes created an unnecessary barrier, hindering some people from receiving my message. She helped me make the necessary alterations. She pointed out the benefit of using examples and illustrations to clarify my key points and encouraged me to shorten my typically lengthy lists of key points.

When Kathy learned I was using short papers and pamphlets (the ones I had sent to the Immigration and Naturalization Service to help people see, from a fact-based perspective, that they could trust the accuracy of the Bible), she asked for some copies. Having just changed jobs from communications and publications at the University of Southern California to teaching freshmen and sophomores at Pasadena City College, she immediately recognized my materials needed some work. Not wanting to insult me, she hesitated, but then gently asked if I'd be open to a little editing of these pieces for clarity and impact. Her face showed surprise and relief when I replied, "Thanks for offering. I'd be grateful."

As it turned out, my interactions with Kathy were beginning to impact her in nearly the same way my relationship with Dave had influenced him. Like Dave, Kathy had been frustrated in her efforts to share her faith with colleagues and others. They refused to listen to the "four laws," and they credited her beliefs to "lifelong indoctrination." She wanted desperately to show them that her faith was rooted in fact, not fiction, but without answers to her brother's science-based challenges, she felt unprepared. Everything changed, she told me, when she heard my story and recognized science as an ally, not an enemy, to faith in Christ.

In all her classes at the college, Kathy began to drop hints about her Christian worldview and indicated her willingness to discuss it outside of class. She noticed that some of her colleagues openly commented on their beliefs—Zen Buddhism, agnosticism, Hinduism, atheism, New Age spirituality, etc. This observation added to her boldness. According to the department chairperson, she could respond to virtually any question or topic a student might raise, as long as she identified it as her "personal perspective." All she lacked, at this point, was practice in communicating biblical truths without church jargon.

That practice did come, but not at all in a way Kathy expected. More on that story in the following pages. For now, I'd like to reveal one of the most startling and humbling encounters of my life.

God's Audible Voice
In my many years of full-time Christian ministry, I've heard many people claim that God "told" them to do certain things or say certain things, but such claims raise cautionary flags for me. Often the actions or words they describe go beyond or even contradict what I read in Scripture. Obviously, the Holy Spirit can and does guide us in making decisions and prompts us to speak up in various circumstances, but we must all be willing to discern whose voice we're really listening to. Sometimes our own deep yearnings speak more loudly than God's voice.

On one occasion, however, I believe I really did hear him speak, loudly and clearly. He spoke audible words I needed to hear. May I never need to hear them again.

A few months before completing my thesis, as I raced to tie up loose ends and prepare for its defense, my supervising professor told me to stop everything and take a time-out to apply for postdoctoral positions as well as for a National Research Council Canada's Postdoctoral Fellowship. Caltech was my first choice, but it seemed a long shot and the fellowship even more so, given that Canada awarded only fifty per year in the physical sciences category. That fellowship included a stipend for the institution that accepted me, which meant that if I received it, I could probably go anywhere in the world to continue my research.

A month later, I heard back from Caltech. They had accepted my application, with or without the fellowship. A month after that, I heard that I had been awarded the fellowship. Caltech invited me for the full three years of postdoctoral studies and arranged for the necessary visa.

As I began my postdoctoral research, my pride began to spin out of control. Everything seemed to be going my way. Here I was meeting and interacting with some of the world's top astronomers. Even the one who had sharply disagreed with some of my research conclusions agreed to collaborate with me. Caltech's Owens Valley Radio Observatory performed better than I could have imagined, and yet I was given the opportunity to work with top computer programmers to further enhance its operation through automation. Meanwhile, in my synthesis of the astrophysical literature, I was seeing new ways to help solve some of the remaining puzzles in the physics of quasars and active galaxies. I had gained respect and acceptance beyond my dreams.

Sometimes our own deep yearnings speak more loudly than God's voice.

Instead of giving God the credit for all these wonderful gifts, I began to credit my own intellect and hard work. How foolish! Everything from my IQ to my physical health and stamina had come to me as a gift. I owed thanks to my parents and especially to my Creator.

One evening alone in my apartment, as I sat reveling in all my so-called accomplishments, an audible voice interrupted my reverie. Loudly, clearly, and emphatically the speaker said, "You are *not* as great as you think you are."

Startled, I looked around the room, and then the truth dawned on me. Who else but God would offer such a stern and timely rebuke? Who else but God would see the danger of my soaring pride and care enough to warn me against it? Who else knew that I could never accomplish his purposes and plans for me unless and until this debilitating sin were cleared out of the way?

I'm convinced nothing less than a dramatic and tangible intervention would have brought me down to earth and down to my knees at that moment. But, in his kindness, God had communicated the horror and repulsiveness of my pride. He called me to repent, which I most certainly did.

Over the next few weeks, as I asked God to help me repudiate pride and grow in humility, he graciously granted me unprecedented opportunities to share my faith with my fellow astronomers. It was then that I realized, and never again forgot, that quasars and galaxies are temporal, but the souls and spirits of human beings are eternal. Yes, God wanted me to study the book of nature—but not for its own sake. He wanted me to use it to bring people to the book of Scripture, inspired by the Source of both books.

If not for God's intervention, I hate to think what I might have become, perhaps an arrogant scientist whom no one would want to listen to. I doubt I would have been willing to consider leaving research and academia for full-time Christian work. Does God ever speak to people in an audible voice? Experience tells me he will, if necessary, to capture our attention and "deliver us from evil."

Revelation 3:19 says, "Those whom I love I rebuke and discipline. So be earnest and repent." Each time I read that verse I recall the time God spoke to me aloud. It makes me grateful for God's ability to read and respond to the attitudes and intents of my heart, keeping me on the path he prepared for me.

Chapter 8

Ready for Anything

The familiar adage "Practice makes perfect (or at least *better*)" applies as much to faith sharing as to virtually any other activity. I've observed an unmistakable synergy between engagement in purposeful, proactive outreach and *serendipitous* encounters with people that lead to spiritually significant conversations. Taking the initiative to present reasons for faith in Christ with people who don't yet know him and who realize we're there for that purpose can enhance our sensitivity and readiness for moments when the Holy Spirit surprises us with such opportunities.

In fact, this preparedness works both ways. Embracing those moments when the Holy Spirit sets up an unexpected encounter fuels our enthusiasm and sharpens our skills in purposeful evangelistic endeavors. A good balance between purposeful and serendipitous outreach involvement brings greater confidence and fluency in explaining the vital truths of the gospel and greater alertness to the core issues holding people back from believing. It also helps us develop greater gentleness, respectfulness, and authenticity, qualities that tend to help people hear and receive our reasons.

Door-to-Door Evangelism

Based on my naive response to Dave's suggestion that I "walk across the street" from Caltech to start sharing evidence for the gospel truth with nonscientists, I discerned that knocking on people's doors might be the most direct way to determine the spiritual status of individuals in any given neighborhood. Obviously, proponents of distorted versions of Christianity were already both active and, to some degree, effective in influencing people's beliefs through knocking on their doors. Why not give it a try?

I don't blame the leaders of our church for their initial resistance to my door-to-door evangelism plans. They had no desire to see our members resemble in-your-face cultists. Neither did I. Perhaps my background in research had something to do with the approach I proposed. Realizing that the development of an effective outreach strategy for our congregation depended upon acquiring good data about the spiritual condition and needs of the various neighborhoods surrounding our church, I suggested going door-to-door with survey questions for each household. Through the survey questions, which could be adapted to fit a given neighborhood's unique characteristics, we hoped to spark spiritual curiosity. And we would always invite the people we surveyed to ask any spiritual questions they wanted.

My statement that this canvassing effort would *not* be used as an occasion to invite church attendance raised additional concerns. However, the pastors and other leaders accepted the reasoning behind this stance: Any hint that we put a higher priority on growing our church than on ministering to them would diminish the evangelistic effectiveness of our effort. So we would focus, instead, on launching home Bible studies within easy walking distance of those surveyed. Of course, if people we talked with asked about our church, we would gladly give them the appropriate information.

Approval was granted, and the door-to-door surveying began. I'm glad to report that several neighborhood Bible studies did get launched. Some grew so large we had to split them into smaller groups. Eventually, a new church emerged from those home Bible studies and new ministries were born.

Initially, however, recruitment proved our biggest challenge. Adult converts overflowing with joy and gratitude for their newfound faith readily stepped forward, but more mature believers hesitated, Kathy included. Dave and I and the eager new Christians prayed for help. Because these new converts lacked depth in their Bible knowledge, they knew they needed to team up with more biblically literate Christians. The new converts could record responses to the survey questions while the older (in the faith) Christians could help in answering biblical or theological questions raised by those we surveyed.

We chose Saturday afternoons as the best time to head into neighborhoods, two by two. At first only one or two teams went out, but through time that number grew to a dozen or more. Nearly every week, someone would pray with a team or two to receive Christ as Lord and Savior. An added thrill came from seeing the effect this outreach had on the longtime believers who participated. Let me tell you about one.

Kathy, the Recruit
After meeting Kathy in a home Bible study, I lost contact with her, except

through her roommate, Michele, who continued to attend. Kathy's new teaching position, which included five English composition classes, took so many hours of preparation and grading she had to drop out of the study for survival's sake. At the same time, her interaction with all these students, so many with spiritual needs and spiritual openness, gave her a longing to become better equipped to speak with them about her faith in Christ.

Given her background in an extended family and multiple generations of believers, not to mention saturated church involvement that included two services on Sundays, prayer meeting and orchestra practice during the week, missions conferences, weddings, and other special events on weekends, Kathy had little practice in talking about her faith with people outside church environments, despite having attended public schools and a secular university and having worked in secular firms. She longed for a way to get some practice. When her roommate mentioned that I had started up a door-to-door survey outreach and recommended it as a way to gain that practice, Kathy responded, "No way." I'll let Kathy tell the rest in her own words:

Any hint that we put a higher priority on growing our church than on ministering to them would diminish the evangelistic effectiveness of our effort.

My flat rejection of the door-to-door outreach, on the excuse that it's somehow "inappropriate," began to bother me more and more, especially as I learned from my roommate, Michele, about the new believers we knew who willingly stepped up. I remembered having told God many times during my growing up years that I'd go anywhere to help bring lost people to faith in him. I asked him to please make it a place with no spiders, but otherwise, anywhere. Now, here I stood, unwilling to drive just a few miles down the road to knock on someone's door. Hmm.

When this inner struggle became too intense to bear, I finally relented. "Okay, Lord, I'll give it a try, at least one time." So, I called for details on where and when to show up, thinking we'd begin with a helpful "how-to" lesson. Instead, we simply prayed, picked up our clipboards, and off we went. As this week's newest trainee, I was paired with Hugh. He remembered me from the Bible study, but he had no idea how nervous I felt—or how relieved when no one answered our knock at the first couple of doors.

At the next house a man was in the driveway, washing his car. When Hugh asked if he could answer a few questions for us, he pointed us toward his front door. His wife was home, and she invited us in to talk. Within minutes Hugh and I discovered she belonged to a Jehovah's Witness congregation. Her aim that day was to convert us!

For the next two hours or so, I became the observer of an intense spiritual ping-pong match. She and Hugh traded Scripture verses back and forth, again and again, she from her notebook, he from the pages of the Old and New Testament. He seemed always to know just where to turn, and I was astounded. I thought, "I should be taking notes on this theology lesson! I should know these verses as well as Hugh does!" I also began thinking about the profound "coincidence" this encounter represented. Could this be God's doing?

My first attempt to share my faith with anyone went back to the day I gave my life to Christ and invited him to live in me. I was five years old, aware of my need for a Savior, and now, having prayed the sinner's prayer, feeling the burst of joy and freedom that comes from receiving a new heart. So, I rushed across the street to tell my six-year-old neighbor all about this great gift. I may have mentioned something about heaven and hell along the way. Whatever the case, the neighbor girl's mother immediately phoned my mother, clearly irritated, requesting that I be kept from speaking to her daughter, disturbing her Jehovah's Witness beliefs. My mom apologized, and I could tell she was embarrassed. I got the message I had done something wrong and felt absolutely crushed. Maybe I should keep my mouth shut from now on, at least if my words made people so upset.

That experience had held me back for twenty years, but I began to break free on this first day of door-to-door visitation. As the conversation ended, I invited the woman to participate in the Bible study just down the street, and we left, presumably headed for the next house. Hugh surprised me by saying it was time to go home. The hours had flown so quickly for me, I could hardly believe my watch. I assured Hugh I'd be back the next week. "Good," he said, "because now that you're experienced, I'll team you with one of the new believers." Had I known the plan, I might not have committed to return, but I couldn't back out now.

Penny picked up a clipboard and walked beside me that following Saturday. She had come to Christ so recently, she had only had time to read the Gospel of John and a portion of Romans, but she was as passionately grateful as I had felt at age five. To my utter amazement, God led us to the door of a teenaged girl who invited us in. She said her parents were out, but she wanted to take our survey.

After going through a few questions, Penny could hold back no longer. She tearfully shared the story of how God had freed her from despair over the mess she had made of her life, and she appealed to this young girl to avoid the kinds of mistakes she had made by giving her life to Christ now. To my greater amazement, the girl said, "I'd like to." Her readiness so caught me off guard that I questioned whether she really understood the magnitude of the commitment she'd be making. After cautiously raising a few more questions, I felt sure. We prayed together and before parting talked further about how she could grow in her relationship with Christ. Penny and I virtually floated back to home base, praising God with all our hearts.

My life changed that day. I experienced the truth that God is ready and willing to use me if and when I am ready and willing to be used. I finally believed in the depths of my soul that he had prepared good works "in advance for us to do" (Ephesians 2:10). I could hardly wait for whatever opportunities he would open up for further practice. And almost immediately he began to bring students into my office at the college with questions about the Bible and about my faith in Christ. At least a few that I know of chose to become his disciples.

One Closed, Five Open

Most of our door-to-door outreach took place in communities either near the church or near a home Bible study. So, when one of our church members urged me to send a team to the neighborhood of one of his nonbelieving coworkers about 20 miles away, I had to tell him we simply lacked the capacity to extend our surveying efforts that far. Finally, after several weeks' resistance to persistent pleading, I relented. I committed to send a team to this coworker's street, but only if this member committed to spend that afternoon praying for us as we went.

That day my survey partner was a young man who'd come to Christ just six weeks earlier. Wanting to avoid the appearance of "targeting," we decided to start at the first house on the block, next door to the coworker's home. There we met a young couple, already Christians, who had lots of questions and encouragement for us. Emboldened, we headed next door, but the response to our knock seemed anything but welcoming. In fact, this man made it abundantly clear he had no interest in taking our survey or conversing with us about anything, period. Though disappointed, we figured why not go ahead and knock on a few more doors.

That's when the real reason for our coming came to light. At three different homes we met people who wanted to take the survey and, more importantly, to talk with us about their doubts and difficulties in believing the Bible. They listened intently and responded with breathtaking openness. One asked us what it takes to become a follower of Christ. Another asked how someone can know for sure that their sins are forgiven. Another wanted to discuss life after death. My young partner and I had the pleasure and privilege of leading all three in a prayer of commitment to Jesus Christ.

With joy I shared with the man who pleaded with us to visit his coworker's street that God used him in a way none of us could have anticipated. Three people had come to Christ thanks to his concern for a coworker and his prayers that afternoon. And now that nonbelieving associate had four neighbors available and willing to continue praying for and reaching out to him. God had something bigger planned than we had envisioned. What a boost to all of us!

God had something bigger planned than we had envisioned.

Comparing Notes

One Saturday afternoon, as our door-to-door teams spread out along the south side of the street, we noticed we weren't the first to arrive. Other teams of two moved from house to house along the north side. We could tell from the literature they carried and a few other clues that they had come to convey a message different from ours, and we wondered how the neighborhood folks might feel about this apparent bombardment.

My partner and I were relieved to meet with doors and hearts wide open. We spent significant time in three homes that day, discussing questions about the existence of God, the identity of Jesus, and how to understand certain troubling passages in the Bible. Rich conversations. When I mentioned having brought with me (attached to my clipboard) a few one- or two-page papers on such topics as fulfilled prophecy and scientific discoveries forecast in the Bible, eager hands reached for them. Needless to say, we enjoyed a wonderful afternoon.

As we exited the last of these three houses, smiling, two individuals from the group working their way along the north side of the street crossed over to confront us, looking puzzled and perplexed. "We arrived before you guys and have covered several blocks along this street, knocking on dozens of doors, and no one has wanted to talk or to accept our literature. What are you doing to get such a different response?"

We let them know we were not selling anything, not even promoting a particular church or denomination, other than inviting people to a local Bible study, if interested. Primarily, we had come to offer people a personal relationship with Jesus Christ and help remove any barriers that might hold them back from receiving it. We also mentioned that we counted on the Holy Spirit to stir up hunger for God in people's hearts and help them recognize the truth about Jesus Christ when they heard it.

We continued to talk briefly about where their beliefs and ours diverged, and we left them with the only two handouts remaining: "The Great Claims of Jesus" and "Barriers to Salvation." We also encouraged them to read through the entire Bible, not just selected verses here and there. They thanked us for the conversation and said they would do as we recommended. I hope and pray we'll find out someday that they did.

Man in the Street

I'm not the only one to remember some of the unusual encounters God gave us on these door-to-door ventures. Patty Bradbury, one of our courageous participants, recounts one that impressed her:

I was a fairly new Christian when I joined a group, led by Hugh, engaged in door-to-door evangelism. The times I participated, we used a "Spiritual Inventory Survey" as a tool to get people talking about spiritual issues. I really liked this tool because it was a good icebreaker and didn't mention any particular church. Also, it started off with very general questions such as "Do you pray?" Most people were pretty open, although (given it was Saturday) we sometimes heard, "I don't have time right now." I don't recall anyone ever being openly hostile, but we did hear some pretty unusual answers at times.

One encounter stands out in my mind. We were just about done for the day, having completed our assigned block. I was in a group with Hugh and another young woman. As we were leaving the last house, I noticed a man on the street, working on his car. It seemed to me he had been there for quite a long while, and I wondered if Hugh would approach him. He did.

The guy looked somewhat intimidating, with long hair, tattoos and (I think) a motorcycle vest. The young woman with us seemed visibly nervous. I don't recall whether Hugh started off with the survey or just started talking cars. The man seemed open and interested in what we were doing. It turns out, he had been watching us, listening to whatever he could hear, and hoping we would approach him because he had lots of questions.

He and Hugh conversed for quite a while, and he asked some really good questions. He remained courteous throughout the interaction, in spite of his "scary" appearance. I don't know if Hugh actually led him to the Lord that day, but he certainly answered a lot of the man's questions. We left him with some material to read, and my own faith was strengthened by the experience. I realized God really does prepare people for us to share his love with, but it might not be exactly who we're expecting.

Teens and Parents

Another team member from those door-to-door outreach days, John Manfro, shares this memorable story:

> **God really does prepare people for us to share his love with, but it might not be exactly who we're expecting.**

I had become a Christian less than a year earlier, and Hugh teamed me up with another guy who also was a relatively new believer. The two of us only got to knock on one door that afternoon.

A couple of teenagers answered our knock. They were especially receptive to our survey questions. Even though their parents weren't home, they invited us in, where we were greeted by a third teenager. For the entire afternoon, they plied us with questions about the Bible and Christianity. Halfway through the afternoon they phoned to invite two more friends to join us. They asked if we could come back the following Saturday to talk further about the Bible and Christianity and wondered if they could invite more friends to join us.

We asked Hugh to come with us that next Saturday, in case we needed help with some of their questions. The following Saturday, we went back on our own to meet with the group that by now included fifteen teenagers. During that third visit, thirteen of the fifteen said they were ready to make a commitment. So my partner and I led those thirteen in a prayer of repentance from sin and in dedication of their lives to Jesus Christ as their personal Creator, Lord, and Savior.

We also had follow-up meetings with the parents of these teenagers. Two of the parents may have been Christians already. The others needed assurance that we were not "shoving the Bible down their sons' and daughters' throats." Before long, these parents began plying us with questions about the Bible and Christianity, just as their kids had.

One of the parents told us he knew the pastor of a church in their community and put us in contact with him. When we met with the pastor and told him of our experience with these young people, he eagerly accepted the ministry of discipling them and their parents in their newfound faith in Jesus Christ while we returned to our ministry of visiting people door-to-door.

Three Women

One of the homes where we formed a Bible study sat only a few blocks from a Kingdom Hall of Jehovah's Witnesses. So before sending out door-to-door teams in that neighborhood, I gave some teaching on core differences between Jehovah's Witness doctrines and the historic Christian beliefs. John Manfro tells the story of what happened a few Saturdays later when he and two friends from the study went out to survey the neighborhood:

The first person to answer our knock seemed impressed that we were going door-to-door to share our Christian faith. She invited us in, where we were greeted by two other ladies. All three identified themselves as relatively new members of the local Kingdom Hall.

We spent an entire afternoon discussing the very topics we had just studied—differences between the doctrines of the Jehovah's Witnesses and the doctrines of Christianity. At the end of the afternoon, the three women said they had more questions and asked if we would be willing to come back the following Saturday afternoon. Of course, we said, "Yes."

The next Saturday, several of the women's friends had come, too. After asking us a few questions, they learned that the three of us were new believers in Christ, and they wanted to hear our stories. As we shared, it became readily apparent that our conversion experiences and the lives we were enjoying since coming to Christ presented a contrast to their experiences in becoming Jehovah's Witnesses.

The whole group invited us to come back the following Saturday for a third meeting. They also asked us if they could bring the lead elder from their Kingdom Hall. We agreed, as long as we, too, could bring one of our home Bible study leaders. They said that would be fine.

That next Saturday, Hugh accompanying us, we met with quite a crowd in that home. Mostly we listened to the dialogue between Hugh and the Jehovah's Witness elder.

The latter insisted that Jesus could not possibly be God since he submitted to "the only God, Jehovah." Hugh pointed out that in Jeremiah 23:5–6, David's righteous Branch, the King from his lineage, was referred to as JHWH (Jehovah). He then asked the elder whether he interpreted the submission of Jesus to the Father as proof that Jesus was less than, that is, inferior to, the Father. The elder said, "Yes."

Hugh then asked the elder if he believed that the Bible taught that wives should submit to their husbands. The elder replied, "Yes." Hugh then asked if the wife's submission implied that women are inferior to men. The elder responded, "Yes."

I could see a sudden change in the faces all around the room. The women were taken aback at hearing their elder declare that women are inferior to men. The meeting ended shortly thereafter, and the three women we had met on our first visit to this home said, "We won't be going to any more meetings at the Kingdom Hall." One of the three soon began attending our Bible study.

As for the others attending that third meeting, they asked if we could come back one more time to answer their questions. We did. This time, no elder came along with them.

Workplace Outreach

My motivation for launching neighborhood outreach, such as door-to-door surveys, sprang from my reading of the New Testament. While Jesus certainly did speak in synagogues on occasion, he focused much or most of his attention on religious outsiders. To me this meant taking the good news to people who lacked any meaningful connection with the church or with Christians. Evangelism most often takes place, and certainly begins, *outside* the church.

With people spending less time at home and more at work or at play, I encouraged members of my Sunday morning class and weeknight Bible studies to consider ways to plant (and nurture) seeds of truth in their workplace. Together we came up with a number of ideas, such as launching a Bible study or reading group during lunch hour or break time at or near work. One person thought to invite a British coworker to read and discuss a C. S. Lewis book, which led to weekly conversations for months. Others came up with even more creative ideas for activities with potential to spark spiritual interest.

For example, a handful of believers who met for Bible study at a large technology firm developed a unique outreach plan for Christmas. Their theme: Christmas foods from around the world. The Bible study members recruited

Christian relatives and friends from a variety of ethnic backgrounds to prepare traditional Christmas treats from their country of origin.

The CEO gave the group permission to use the largest meeting room in the building to display and serve these foods—a table for each country. At each table, a sign identified the country and a poster or handout explained how the food symbolized or otherwise connected with some aspect of the [biblical] Christmas story.

Pleased to see the morale boost this special event had generated, the CEO approved the group's additional request. They could invite a scientist to give a brief talk after lunch about how such a variety of tasty, colorful foods came to be possible. This talk on Earth's fine-tuning for humanity's benefit led to a "boss-approved" Q&A session and many more "divine design" discussions for weeks afterward. Those Bible study members who most easily and enjoyably participated in these discussions had gained confidence from their practice in our door-to-door outreach.

Evangelism most often takes place, and certainly begins, *outside* the church.

More than Chance

After each Saturday afternoon survey outing, those who participated met for a debriefing session. During those times, team members would rejoice together and pray for those people with whom we had interacted. As the weeks and months rolled on, we began to notice how many times our single moms ended up speaking with other single moms, car enthusiasts with auto aficionados, salesmen with salespeople, teachers with either students or fellow teachers, and in my case, with engineers and scientists. On one particular Saturday, the only people I talked with were engineers and scientists, while no one else on any of our teams had encountered a single engineer or scientist.

Could this high rate of affinity connection result from mere chance—as when Dodgers fans gravitate toward other Dodgers fans or jeep owners start seeing jeeps everywhere? Given the random way we assigned teams to different sections of a neighborhood, pure coincidence seemed too big a stretch. Something more than chance had been guiding our encounters.

When these and other outreach activities began drawing more and more people to visit our church each Sunday, I realized the need and the opportunity to follow up with these visitors to discover ways we could serve them and incorporate them in the life of our congregation. Each week the pastor encouraged newcomers to fill out a card from the rack in front of them and drop it in the offering plate when it passed by. Cards with a check mark in the "visitor" box came to me, and on Tuesday evenings several volunteers, including some longtime church members, joined me in going by twos or threes to visit the visitors. Just as with our door-to-door Saturdays, these Tuesday nights led to many a thrilling encounter.

Jackie's Story
To encourage participation, I would often choose one or two stories from these Tuesday visits to share with the Sunday morning congregation. For a few church members, these stories raised more skepticism than eagerness. I'll let one of the skeptics, an artist named Jackie Stewart, speak for herself:

Hugh would give a two-minute report every Sunday morning about how God had enabled one or more participants in our church's outreach ministries either to see a spiritual breakthrough or to lead a nonbeliever to faith in Jesus Christ. One Sunday, I could no longer swallow my incredulity, and I confronted Hugh. While I granted that a few of his stories might be true, I said there was no way they could all be accurate. I was convinced, and I told him so, that he must be greatly exaggerating.

Hugh let me know he had not intended to convey that every member of the teams experienced a dramatic event every week. Hugh explained that while one or two team members would typically see something amazing, the others might not. I remained skeptical, and I said so. After all, with only a couple of dozen people at most going out each week, the number of these breakthroughs seemed impossibly high.

At this point, Hugh challenged me to put his credibility to the test. He invited me to join one of our evangelism teams to see for myself. I elected to join the team that followed up with first-time visitors to our church.

On my first Tuesday evening, I was teamed up with Hugh. He always went with the "newbie." As we approached the first address, Hugh cautioned me not to expect a miracle on our first call. He suggested it might take six to eight visits before anything truly remarkable happened.

Within minutes an engineering student answered the door and asked us to come in. He told us he had just become convinced that a God must exist, a God who created the universe, very likely the God Christians believe in. He said, "I visited your church hoping to have these beliefs confirmed and to find out what to do about them."

Hugh took a few minutes to describe how recent scientific discoveries affirmed the reality of a God beyond space and time who had not only brought the universe into existence but had also fine-tuned it to fulfill his purposes and plans for humanity. I jumped in to say that all humans need a Redeemer to atone for their offenses against God (and others) and to enter an eternal, personal relationship with God. Hugh briefly reviewed evidence that Jesus of Nazareth is the Redeemer. Then, I asked the young man if he was ready to repent of his sins, receive God's redemptive offer, and trust Jesus Christ as his own Savior and Lord.

He answered with a solemn, "Yes." So I led him in a prayer of repentance and dedication of his life to Christ, his Redeemer and Master. As you may guess, the next Sunday I had to tell everyone I'd been wrong to doubt Hugh's stories. I had seen for myself that the Holy Spirit is eager to work through us if we only show up and let him. I urged everyone to get in on the action.

That first Tuesday evening was only the beginning. In the weeks, months, and years to follow, I saw God at work again and again. I learned from Hugh to ignore distractions, including (at times) "Beware of Dog" signs. This may sound strange, but I can't tell you how often the so-called "dangerous" dog would pave the way for us to talk with someone who needed spiritual help.

The Silent Guard Dog

One Tuesday evening, a young man who'd been a follower of Christ for just a few years came to participate in a follow-up visitation. As a first-timer, he accompanied me. That night, we zoomed through our stack of cards because no one answered our knock on their door. Our stack dwindled to just one card.

We followed our Thomas Guide (a spiral-bound street map used in pre-smartphone days) to a large property surrounded by a high wall with an equally high gate. We tried the latch, which opened easily, and a large German shepherd greeted us. The dog then herded us gently along a dark path about a hundred yards or so to the front door of a house. In answer to my knock, the door burst open and the man of the house exclaimed, "How did you get here? Did you not see the sign?" Before we could ask, "What sign?" he blurted, "You must be from the church!"

The man invited us in and introduced us to his wife and three children. He told us that over dinner earlier that evening, his family had asked God to send them someone who could explain what it means to be a Christian. With the German shepherd leaning calmly against my left leg, I explained that because of who Jesus is and what he did for us on the cross before rising bodily from the dead, anyone can enjoy an eternal loving relationship with God. All we need do is repent of our sin, accept Jesus's payment of sin's consequence on our behalf, and submit to Jesus Christ the Master of our life. Without hesitation, all five family members prayed with me that evening to begin their new life in Jesus Christ.

After talking further about how to grow in this new relationship, the family wanted to explain what a miracle our arrival at their door represented. First, they told us they had reason for the fence, the gate, and the sign out front. When they visited the church and filled out the card, they thought someone might phone them, but they never imagined someone would simply show up. They asked why the sign that warned of a trained attack dog hadn't kept us from opening the gate. We told them we saw no such sign. Later, when we left, we confirmed it hung there, big and bold, and yet invisible to us when we had arrived.

They went on to describe their German shepherd's specialized training. He did not allow anyone to approach the gate without barking loudly. If any intruder dared to open the gate, he would grab an arm or a leg and hold on, just as a police dog would. Knowing that the dog allowed us to enter and guided us to the front door convinced this man and his family that God had heard and miraculously answered their plea. The sight of the dog sitting beside me as I explained the gospel sealed the conclusion. He had never sat close to anyone but the five of them.

Eager to remove any doubt from our minds that a miracle had occurred, the man proceeded to show us exactly how well trained the shepherd was. He gave a command, and the dog hurried out to the hen house, rousted out the three roosters, nudged a hen off her egg, softly clenched the egg in his powerful jaw, and placed it, unscathed, in a basket beside the back door, continuing to fill the basket until the man signaled him to stop.

We believed.

We headed back to the church, at first too awestruck for words. Who would believe our account of this evening? It seemed surreal, even to us! My teammate's comment best summed it up: "The book of Acts really is true!"

Warlock's Escapee
One of the most disturbing calls I made during those years of follow-up

visitation took me into a neighborhood I later learned from a detective friend even the police hesitated to go. As we approached the door, a sickening stench nearly pushed us back. A man opened the door and we asked for the woman whose name appeared on our card.

"She's mine," he hissed, "and so are these others," he added, pointing toward other women lurking in the room's shadowy corners. "I can make them do anything I want, and you can't do anything about it!" When I asked again to speak with the person whose name appeared on the card in my hand, he said, "See that girl in the street? I can make her do a cartwheel if I want." To prove his powers, he mumbled unintelligibly and the girl immediately performed a cartwheel. "Shall I do it again?" he asked.

I said, "No."

He turned toward the women and commanded them not to listen to us. Turning back to me he sneered, "I know the Bible better than you do, better than any so-called *believer*. Name any chapter and verse of the New Testament and I'll quote it for you, forward and backward."

I countered, "Pick any New Testament passage you want, and tell us what it means." Flustered, he asked us to leave immediately. I said I would return "if and when" he wanted to talk about what the words he had memorized actually mean.

Sometime later, I learned the story behind that evening's visit. This warlock had been holding six women captive, ensnared by his demonic powers. They lived in terror and had nearly lost all hope of escaping his grip. On a particular Sunday, one of them fled the house while the others distracted him. She told me she had no idea how she made it to our church, but when she got there, she dashed inside, scribbled her name and address on a card, dropped it on the nearest seat, and rushed back, trembling.

She said my visit, just two days later, had unnerved her captor. His inability to respond to my challenge so disturbed him that he began to lose his hold on her, and also on the other five women. Eventually, they all escaped, and though she had no knowledge of what happened to the others, she was trying to rebuild her life. She was grateful for the help of some Christian women she had met.

Blockade Breakthrough

I may not have mentioned that my position as minister of evangelism also encompassed oversight of our church's missions outreach and missionaries. For the latter, I received significant help from a dedicated Missions Commission.

On occasion, this group deemed it necessary for either our pastor or me (or both) to make a field visit, and because of my unique background, these overseas visits sometimes led to unusual opportunities for me.

One such opportunity came from a university campus ministry in Durban, South Africa—during the apartheid era. On our way to the campus for my open-to-all lecture on scientific evidences for the God of the Bible, the student organizers warned me that a major protest had begun that morning. A strike threatened to shut down every class—my speaking event, included.

As we approached the lecture hall, we noticed muscular guards barricading all entrances. They said, "Your event is canceled. You must leave."

Unwilling to let this opportunity slip through my fingers, I decided to take a page from the book of Daniel and make an appeal. Even though the encounter occurred three decades ago, I can vividly recall the conversation. I let them know I had come from the United States to give this talk, that the talk had been planned and scheduled seven months earlier, and that I had no connection whatsoever to the university administration or any other political entity. I invited them to review the outline of my talk, if that would ease their concerns.

They took me up on the offer and, to my surprise, asked if I could come back at a later date, *after* the protest. My hosts explained that rescheduling by the two or three weeks they suggested was impossible (because I was booked solid for the remainder of my time in southern and eastern Africa) and that the event must take place *that day*. In response to this apparent impasse, the guards resorted to pushing us away, physically, from the main door. Just then I heard an inner voice say, "Let *them* speak, too."

Backing away from their powerful arms, I asked, "What if we both speak?" They paused for a moment as I outlined a proposal: "You speak for ten minutes and invite everyone either to leave with you in protest or to stay and hear what I have come to say. If everyone leaves, I'll leave too, but if even one person stays, you allow me to stay and give my message." I also promised to make no negative comments about them or their protest. After a brief discussion among themselves, the men agreed.

Soon students *and* faculty began to pour into the lecture hall. Curious onlookers hung around just outside the doors. As I stood to one side, five protestors took the stage. Their leader seized the microphone and began to recite a long list of the administration's "evil" deeds. He punctuated his presentation with shouts, "They must be stopped!" In an emotional pitch, he urged everyone to walk out and to stay out of class until certain demands were met.

As the five marched toward the door, two students joined them.

Meanwhile, the crowd outside decided to come inside to see what had caused such a commotion, not realizing it had nothing to do with me, really. I'd estimate curiosity, alone, brought an additional two hundred students and faculty, not to mention reporters from the campus newspaper.

They gave me their full attention, and with the disruption to the day's class schedule, no one seemed in a rush to leave. Questions and discussion extended long into the afternoon, and the campus ministry leaders connected with many who expressed interest in further conversation. As in the book of Acts, what threatened to thwart the spread of the gospel led to greater impact than anyone dared to imagine.

The Lawyer and His Family

On another occasion, my pastoral position took me on a trip with one of our missionaries to Slovenia, Croatia, and Serbia, what was then the Communist country of Yugoslavia. As we crossed the border from Austria, border guards searched in and under our car for contraband. The items of greatest concern: guns and Bibles.

The highlight of this trip was a "quiet" event in Ljubljana, Slovenia. Our sponsors packed chairs into the two rooms that served as our venue and soon all seats were taken. All the remaining space was filled with people standing and a few seated on the floor in front of me. Among the last people to squeeze in was a well-known lawyer—a Communist party member, most likely. We learned later that he and his wife and their two teen-aged children had spent an entire month's gasoline allowance to attend the event. The four of them had to sit in different parts of the two rooms where they could not see each other.

As in the book of Acts, what threatened to thwart the spread of the gospel led to greater impact than anyone dared to imagine.

I knew that the Yugoslavian population had been inundated with atheistic propaganda, assertions that science had disproved God's existence and that the Bible could not be true. The missionary urged me to emphasize as much as I could through a translator that science firmly establishes the existence of God and the complete reliability and trustworthiness of the Bible.

My message and the Q&A session that followed deeply moved the audience. Tears of joy flowed down many faces. Many prayed with me to commit their lives to Jesus Christ as their Savior and Lord.

As the gathering began to disperse, I saw the lawyer and his family talking nervously near the door, where they had now come together. The translator and I approached to see if something was wrong and if we might be of help. We learned that each of the four had prayed with me and felt worried about telling the other three. The tension quickly gave way to unspeakable joy. The family's response dramatically impacted everyone else in that room, including the missionary, the translator, and me.

Software Engineers

As our church continued to grow, more people heard about the "scientist turned pastor" and wanted to hear my story. A Christian software engineer, originally from Southern California, invited me to speak at a lunch he was planning for colleagues in the San Francisco Bay Area's burgeoning Pleasanton Valley. He thought they might appreciate my fact-based approach.

Nearly all of the 100+ lunch guests worked in high-tech firms, writing code for various new computer applications. Their language: logic. So, I presented an overview of what I considered the best scientific evidence for the biblical Creator and for the supernatural accuracy and authority of the Bible. I showed them evidence that had convinced me and additional evidence accumulated since then. After responding to their astute questions, I invited whoever was ready to acknowledge Jesus Christ as Creator, Lord, and Savior and to entrust their past, present, and future to him, to pray with me. In closing I asked those who had made this commitment to indicate so by checking a box on a card received from the event's organizer.

The response can only be described as unprecedented. Roughly four of every five engineers in attendance who were not already Christians either checked that box or requested more information about what it means to follow Jesus Christ. Those I spoke with afterward told me they had never considered science as an ally to the Christian faith. Now that they understood the rational, logical case for trusting in the Bible and its message, they saw no reasonable or desirable alternative to doing so. In fact, God's offer appeared *optimal*, and optimization is the aim of every computer programmer.

Santa Ana CBMC

Around the same time as this Pleasanton Valley event, the Santa Ana chapter of the Christian Businessmen's Connection (CBMC) invited me to speak at their annual Christmas outreach, one of their largest. They provided clear guidelines about sharing my story without Christian "jargon," given that half the guests would be CBMC members' not-yet-believing business associates, and yet they wanted God's offer of rescue to come across with simple clarity. I could tell some felt tense about the science side of my background, while others, about the pastor side.

With their tension adding to mine, I enlisted an army of pray-ers to back me up, and I could tell as I spoke that the Holy Spirit was speaking through me, guiding my words to their intended mark in men's hearts. Once again, the response exceeded all expectations and led to great rejoicing, as well as many more invitations to speak. It also led to an unexpected conversation with the fellow pastors and lay leaders of my church—a conversation that echoed what God had been hinting at through close family members, friends, and my bride, Kathy.

Wrestling with God

The story of Jacob's wrestling with God all night long became mine when my church leaders challenged me to leave the security of my job with the church for the purpose of launching a wider evangelistic and equipping ministry. At the time, they had no idea Kathy's aunt and uncle and two close friends from one of our home Bible studies had already broached the subject with us, privately, and committed to pray. I acknowledged that such a change posed huge risks for my soon-to-be family. (Kathy and I had just learned our first child was on the way.)

We all realized opposition to such a venture would be strong—both from outside and inside the body of Christ. Skeptics would challenge my credibility for having left a career in research, and many creationists would challenge my salvation and my motives for giving credence to science. To be honest, none of us anticipated the magnitude of the opposition, especially from within the Christian community. I needed a plan, one that would offer at least some possibility of a newly launched ministry's survival beyond a year. I also needed Kathy's wholehearted "yes" to such a venture. The risks would be hers, as well.

Like Jacob, I spent an entire night wrestling with God in prayer for the answers and assurance I needed. Doubts lingered about my readiness to make another career change of such magnitude, this time affecting more than just my own trajectory. Kathy understood my tossing and turning and prayed with me and for me. As the Sun began to peek above the horizon, my thoughts began to clear. Finally I could picture the initial steps of a plan God was laying before me. As a bonus, the Spirit also showed me names and faces of various people he was raising up to come alongside us, people with the knowledge, skills, and other essential resources we lacked. In her mind's eye, Kathy saw Peter stepping out of the boat, staying atop the waves as long as his eyes remained fixed on Jesus.

Together we agreed, "Okay, Lord, we're ready."

Chapter 9

Ready for the Road

With the launch of Reasons to Believe came new opportunities and new challenges. Again, I could see how God had gone ahead of Kathy and me to prepare us. We realized that two years earlier, he had blessed us with a "mailing list" that went beyond our personal Christmas card list. Thousands of people had responded to my interview on Dr. James Dobson's *Focus on the Family* radio program. Dr. Dobson's staff passed along more than 300 listeners' letters posing science-related questions too technical for them to answer and asked that we respond. To complete that task had taken us the better part of a year, but those names and addresses gave us a list of potentially "interested persons."

Friends stepped up to help with every aspect of our work. First, they helped us assemble a prayer team, one that continues to this day. The church allowed us to rent 700 square feet of office space. They generously provided a phone line and covered my salary for a year, in addition to maintaining my health insurance plan. Volunteers stuffed information packets for people who called or wrote with questions. They also duplicated cassette tapes of my outreach talks for distribution. One friend kept the books by hand, another set up outreach events on nearby community college campuses, business and ministry leaders formed a board of directors, and other friends provided childcare so that I could complete my first book and Kathy could produce newsletters and other communications. As the saying goes, "It takes a village," and then some.

As the ministry grew beyond the local area, travel became more frequent and far-reaching for me. My travels added weight to Kathy's shoulders, but the joy of seeing God at work, drawing more and more people to himself and mobilizing even more for outreach, buoyed her up and glued us together. We had seen evidence of divine intervention many times before launching Reasons to Believe, and now we hoped to see even more.

Soviet Lab

At the first inklings of perestroika in the late 1980s, a communist consortium called, simply, the Soviet Lab invited me (nudged by some influential American believers) along with a small cadre of Christian scholars, to three major cities—Moscow, Leningrad (now Saint Petersburg), and Kiev, to speak *only* to scientists and communist party leaders. Soviet officials warned us that to speak with anyone outside their "authorized" venues would mean prompt deportation and no chance of return, ever.

They set other conditions, as well. They told each of us to submit a list of the lectures we would be prepared to present, a list that included both purely scientific talks and talks that integrated science with our Christian beliefs. For each of the speaking events, the assembly of scientists and party personnel would be allowed to choose which talk they wanted to hear.

Knowing the Soviet Union's strong commitment to atheism, I wondered why the Soviet Lab would fund any presentations linking science and Christianity. I learned that the Soviet researchers had shown keen interest in this connection when attending science conferences in the West. In the interest of keeping these brilliant minds at home, the Soviet Lab decided to appease them by bringing us in.

Found in Translation

My first Lab-sponsored talks would be delivered to various research groups in Kiev, Ukraine. The audiences always chose the most overtly Christian talks on my list—talks on scientific evidence for the existence and actions of the God of the Bible and for the scientific accuracy of the biblical creation texts.

Moments before the first event was to begin, three professional translators and a small group of Communist party leaders called me into a side room to determine who would translate my talks. Each of the three professional translators insisted he or she lacked the ability. The party men seemed flummoxed at first, then furious.

To calm things down, I let them know I was not expecting simultaneous translation. Phrase-by-phrase translation, given the nature of my subject matter, seemed the most practical. I also suggested that perhaps all three together could manage the task. The translators, overhearing my comments, firmly maintained their stance. They could not do it.

Tensions rose again until a tall young man in his mid-twenties stepped forward. He explained to me, in English, that the three professional translators feared failure and the loss of their jobs. He then offered, "I may be less polished than they, but I'm not afraid to try." The young man had played basketball on Russia's national team and had "picked up some English" during his travels. I told the party men, "I'd rather work with a translator who's confident than with three who are not."

Reluctantly, they agreed to let the basketball player translate for me and even offered to pay him for his efforts, which certainly pleased him. As the two of us walked into that first afternoon's session, my eyes were drawn to the gigantic (20-foot by 20-foot) portrait of Lenin that would loom over me as I spoke. My translator told me the scientists filing through the door had gathered here every week for years for a two-hour lecture on atheism, considered the foundation for all their science research endeavors.

I noticed that the first four rows had been roped off. These seats, my new friend informed me, belonged to the dignitaries who'd be coming, Ukraine's Communist Party brass. He said, "When you finish your speech, you must answer their questions first."

With boldness built on tested trust in God's faithfulness, I launched into my presentation of astronomical evidences for God's existence and for his precise design of the universe for the benefit of humanity. Whenever my translator tripped over a term or concept, a member of the audience intervened. After all, much of the astronomical literature is published in English. As I ended, several hands went up in the first few rows. The dignitaries wanted to know why, then how, I had become a Christian. I heard these same two questions every time I spoke during this trip.

The morning after my fourth talk, I noticed dark circles under my translator's eyes. He looked exhausted. I asked him, "Are you okay? Did something happen?"

He told me he'd been up most of the night. When I probed a bit further, he told me his entire extended family had gathered at his uncle's place to learn what I had been saying to the scientists. They wanted to know everything, including what questions were being asked and how I answered. Then they asked him to lead them in a prayer of committing their lives to Jesus Christ.

"Did you?" I asked.

"Yes."

"Have you given your life to Christ?"

"My uncle and several of my relatives have, but for me, not yet," he replied. However, after every talk from then on, he peppered me with questions before heading home. He said my answers would help him answer his relatives' nightly quizzing. I could tell he suffered from sleep deprivation, but he no longer seemed to mind.

I spoke in many different lecture halls to many different groups of scientists on this trip, always with Lenin's portrait behind me. Eventually, my basketball-player-turned-translator began introducing me with a nod to the portrait, saying in Russian, "For seventy years, *this* has been our God." Then, he would point to me and say, "Now, Dr. Hugh Ross will tell us about the *real* God."

After my next few talks, when people asked how I had become a Christian or how they could become a Christian, my translator assured me, "You don't need to say anything, Dr. Ross. I can take it from here." Finally, just a few days before the trip ended, he let me know the gospel had finally sunk into his soul and he could now declare himself a follower of Jesus Christ.

> **The gospel had finally sunk into his soul and he could now declare himself a follower of Jesus Christ.**

Russian Philosophers

Before my arrival in Kiev, a local philosophy club heard I would be addressing researchers there and asked if I'd be allowed to speak to them, as well. The Soviet Lab officials granted permission for two talks.

The atmosphere in the meeting hall for that first talk felt heavy, almost physically weighted by a mixture of despair and hostility. Even my translator sensed it, with a slight shiver. As I began to speak, some club members interrupted, shouting loudly in both Russian and English. They lobbed vile obscenities about the character of Jesus Christ. To me their language and behavior strongly suggested demonic interference.

When I later learned that several of these individuals had held professorships in government-sanctioned departments of occult research, I thought, *how ironic.* In American academia, I face the challenge of persuading researchers that a supernatural realm exists. In the (then) Soviet Union, belief in the supernatural proved astonishingly pervasive. Sadly, my Soviet audiences knew only of the dark, enslaving side of that realm.

Amid the obscene and angry outbursts, I detected God's leading me to go straight to questions and answers. I announced I would address any question about science, the Bible, and Christianity. No more speeches today, from me or from anyone else. If someone wanted to rant, I would ignore them and go on to someone with a question. Soon two of the loudest interrupters left the room. Another stayed and to everyone's amazement remained silent.

Within minutes my audience began to listen with rapt attention to the questions raised and the answers given. The changed behavior of that one unruly individual seemed to carry a profound impact. Slowly but surely the subject turned toward who Jesus really is and what Christianity teaches about the meaning of life. The heaviness gave way to hope and even a touch of excitement. The time seemed right to transition from formal questions and answers to informal interaction with individuals and small clusters.

An American colleague with me that day held a master's degree in philosophy. So, while I engaged those with science and Bible questions, mostly in English, I deployed him (with our translator's help) to handle philosophical questions, mostly expressed in Russian. Afterward we thanked God for the remarkable openness and receptivity of those we spoke with.

The next morning, we prepared for my second talk. First, we prayed, and then we formed a plan that seemed wise to both of us. My colleague would sit at the back of the lecture hall and pray throughout my message, calling on the Lord to nullify any more demonic disruptions. As he prayed, I would build a clear and thorough case not only for the Creator's existence, but also for his redeeming love, made available through Christ.

The previous day's antagonists showed up for my second talk, but this time they remained quiet. The presence of a greater power became evident to all, and again the audience showed intense interest. Most of the questions in this second session focused on how anyone can know for sure that the Holy Spirit lives within, guiding them into truth and making transformation possible. My colleague and I couldn't have asked for a more thrilling response, and yet more thrills (and a few chills) awaited.

Russian General

The next day, another researcher from our little group of invited academics gave a technical lecture to a group of chemists and medical science researchers. During the time devoted to fielding questions, one of the chemists asked him, in English, "Are you a Christian?"

"Yes," he said.

"Why?" the chemist asked.

The chief scientist/Communist official in charge of the institute allowed him to answer but soon put an end to the meeting and ordered everyone back to their labs and classes. Loud murmuring rumbled through the lecture hall. A four-star general initiated a tense dialogue with the chief. Our translator seemed too intent on listening to help us understand, but we could tell the temperature was rising. So was my concern because the general kept pointing directly at me. Two of my colleagues feared I might be facing expulsion.

Suddenly, the room fell silent. The general motioned me, with that same hand, toward the podium. Only then did our translator fill us in. Apparently, the general had caught wind of my talk at the philosophers' meeting the day before and made a special trip, along with many others, to hear that same talk *today*. He wanted me to repeat it and told the head scientist to cancel the morning's classes so all the chemists could come. The lab chief wanted a compromise: strictly voluntary attendance. The general's emphatic response, "Nyet."

With my translator's help, I spoke on what the general requested—beginning with what I considered the best scientific evidences for the existence of the God of the Bible and then moving on to his expressed purpose and plan for humanity's redemption. Questions and discussion extended throughout the rest of the morning and into the lunch hour, primarily focused on God's attributes, how we can know for sure what those attributes are, and what they mean for us, personally. Again, the good news went forth, and the results belong to the Lord.

Russian Physicists

These events with philosophers, astronomers, chemists, and other researchers in Kiev preceded a similar event in Moscow. That's where seven hundred physicists gathered to hear about astronomy, physics, and God. I began through a translator giving an overview of how new discoveries in astronomy and physics established the existence of a personal God who transcended time and space and designed the entire universe and fashioned our galaxy, planetary system, and planet for the specific benefit of human beings. Christian philosopher Dr. William Lane Craig followed me with an overview of some of the philosophical arguments for God and a summary of the historical evidence for the bodily resurrection of Jesus from the dead.

During the Q&A that followed our talks, one of the physicists asked me if science played a role in my becoming a Christian and, if so, what role. In my answer, I described how my studies in astronomy had convinced me God must exist, even though my parents and everyone else I knew disagreed. I went on to tell how I searched for this God in the writings of the great philosophers, then in the holy books of the Eastern religions, and finally in a careful study of the Bible I'd picked up at my public school. After summarizing the biblical content that had convinced me this book came from the One who created the universe, I held up that well-worn Gideon Bible, showing my signature on the back page. That's how I had long ago indicated my commitment to Jesus Christ as my personal Savior and Lord.

At this point, I strongly sensed God wanted me to ask the audience a question. "Would you like us to lead you in a prayer of commitment to Jesus Christ right now? You can make him your own Lord and Savior today, if you are ready." Almost all the heads in the auditorium nodded. So, we prayed.

After praying, Dr. Craig and I encouraged all who had prayed with us, if willing, to make a public declaration of their commitment. They could do so by signing their name on a piece of paper and sending it up to the table in front of the podium. Unaware of a temporary paper shortage, we caused a near riot as physicists scrambled to get their hands on even the tiniest scrap. Those who had a piece of paper graciously ripped it into shreds for others. Within minutes a foot-high pile of minuscule paper fragments rose on that table. God alone knows how many physicists gave their lives to him that day.

> **One of the physicists asked me if science played a role in my becoming a Christian . . . my studies in astronomy had convinced me God must exist.**

Men in Black

Meanwhile, at the back of the auditorium stood two men in dark suits next to another table, this one with some boxes stacked on it. As the paper pile grew up front, I noticed a line forming near the back door. The two men who looked like agents (from a distance) were now handing out small books to those who were leaving.

When the auditorium finally emptied, the two men approached me, beaming, and introduced themselves as members of Gideons International. They asked, "Do you remember a Gideons event you spoke at in Santa Barbara a few years ago?" I assured them I did.

"That night we raised funds for foreign languages Bibles," they told me, "specifically Russian language Bibles. The money from that evening covered the cost of all the Bibles we just handed out, and then some!" These men expressed how thrilled they felt to deliver those Bibles personally.

"You should have seen the men's faces," they said, "many with tears streaming. We'll never forget this experience!" Neither will I.

Hotel Visitor

Thanks to these Gideons, each member of our team now packed a few Russian Bibles. We intended to use them as gifts for our translators or to place in other desperate hands, as God directed—secretly, of course. During that era, even pastors had difficulty finding Bibles for purchase, nor could they afford one, when they did. The purchase price at that time equaled two months' wages.

A night or two later, at half past midnight, my American colleague and I heard a faint knock on our hotel room door. I opened it a crack to see a diminutive babushka (elderly Russian woman) standing there, holding a small book in her hand. Clearly she spoke no English, and though I usually fail at charades, I made an effort to discern what she wanted.

Gesturing emphatically, she pointed to the nondescript book in her hand and then toward the desk inside the hotel room, repeating her actions as I struggled to grasp her meaning.

"Bible?" I whispered.

She responded with a vigorous nod as I went to the desk to retrieve one for her. By the time I returned and placed it in her trembling fingers, tears dripped from her chin.

Bowing again and again, she cried softly, "*Spasibo, spasibo, spasibo*" (meaning "thank you"). Then she vanished down the hallway.

Buddhist Professor

In more recent years, as the RTB team has grown, God has opened doors in many more countries—Australia, Brazil, Cambodia, Canada, China, Estonia, Hungary, Honduras, Hong Kong, Japan, Kenya, Lesotho, Mexico, Mongolia, Peru, South Africa, Swaziland, Thailand, Trinidad, Turkey, the United Kingdom, and Zimbabwe, thus far. With each trip God gives fresh opportunities to observe the blessing that comes from readiness to answer questions with gentleness and respect.

One of the many stories that stand out in my memory occurred on my visit to China, where I was invited to address students and faculty at an international school. The government allowed instruction on the Bible and Christianity, given that only expatriates and diplomats' sons and daughters comprised the student body. What a pleasure to interact with these bright young people discussing the connections between science and Scripture and the meaning of faith! As I engaged with students, a few faculty members worked behind the scenes through key contacts to arrange an impromptu outreach event at the nearby university.

God gives fresh opportunities to observe the blessing that comes from readiness.

With just a few hours' notice, via word of mouth, a translator came forward (a Chinese Christian physicist) and a room was cleared of desks to allow for maximum attendance. People of all descriptions poured silently into the cramped space and spilled over into the hallway. As usual, I spoke of my journey to faith and shared some of the most compelling scientific evidence supporting the case for Christ. When I invited questions, one man seemed to dominate. He posed one question after another, with intense emotion. When I expressed concern, my translator waved it away. I kept answering as succinctly as I could and finally prevailed upon the translator to take a question from one or two others who'd been waiting.

As soon as I finished, the man stood abruptly and launched into a monologue. After four or five minutes, I turned again to my translator, wondering what we should do. He whispered, "Let him continue. It's all right." Soon the man wrapped up his message, and smiling eyes lit up the darkening room. As the room quietly emptied, my translator filled me in.

Our intense guest, a Buddhist scholar and professor at the university, had held six major objections to Christianity, objections to which he could find no answers. Apparently, I touched upon some of them in my presentation, and when the opportunity for questions came, he raised the rest. During his "speech," he explained all this to the audience and announced that because I had answered each of his objections, he could no longer remain a Buddhist. He now chose to follow Jesus Christ, instead.

As the translator shared this information with me, I saw the former Buddhist conversing with an older man near the door. Then he turned to me and in broken English thanked me profusely for coming. He assured me he meant what he had said. In fact, as I learned through our translator, the man he had just spoken with was the pastor of a house church and had agreed to baptize him the very next day. I have no doubt whose message carried the greatest impact on all who attended our spur-of-the-moment event.

Mongolian Teachers

The spiritual thaw that accompanied Soviet perestroika expanded to other regions of the world, including the once tightly closed nation of Mongolia. At the earliest signs of this thawing, South Korean Christians entered Mongolia but quickly realized that the country's leaders and teachers had been saturated, even more thoroughly than their Russian counterparts, in scientific atheism. The urgent need and God-given opportunity for Christians to bring credible scientific evidences for the truth claims of the Bible and its offer of redemption became obvious.

An energetic leader in the Campus Crusade for Christ International ministry, Warren Willis, recognized this opportunity and arranged for me to spend a week in Mongolia's capital city, Ulaanbaatar, giving science-based lectures to educators. A young Mongolian woman, who had recently earned a biochemistry degree and had come to know Christ in the United States, agreed to be my translator.

In preparation for my coming, a translation team produced and then broadcast a Mongolian language version of *Journey toward Creation*, the first documentary produced by Reasons to Believe. The team grew so excited to see it, they expanded their plan for the use of my time. They proposed a series of twenty lectures on different science-faith topics and offered to arrange for every teacher in the country to participate. They wanted my outlines and visuals immediately, for the sake of the translator. How could anyone say no to a once-in-a-lifetime opportunity such as this?

The day I arrived, exhausted from having worked on the plane and in airports on this greatly expanded lecture series, the organizers mercifully allowed me to rest through the premiere showing of *Journey toward Creation* in the capitol's largest auditorium. Its 800 sold-out seats held many (perhaps most) of the country's political leaders and other professionals, including many of the teachers. Producers from Mongolia's only television network also attended. The film's message literally stunned the audience.

The next morning, my teaching series launched in the same auditorium, and the television crew returned. After each of the week's lectures, my translator and I sensed increasing receptivity. We could tell from the intense, in-depth questions after each session that the Holy Spirit was opening hearts and minds to the best news these precious people had ever heard. Along with everyone involved in putting this outreach together, we rejoiced. I found it hard to leave at the end of that week, and I thank God for those, including Warren, who stayed behind for follow-up and ongoing ministry. Later, I learned that within six months after my visit, the national television network twice broadcast my entire lecture series and *Journey toward Creation*. So, in one sense, God did allow me to stay. He's still bringing people to himself in that country.

A Common Misconception

At universities around the world, including here in the US and Canada, prevailing opinion says Christianity and science do not, and should not, mix. In fact, Christianity is widely considered *anti*-science. Unless we believers prepare a gracious response to this opinion, we run the risk of affirming it.

Three minutes into my talk at a midwestern American university, a professor rose to his feet to shut me down. He loudly warned students that this Christian speaker would try to sell them a pack of lies. "I'll prove it," he announced, as some in the audience moaned and others tried to shush him.

Turning to me, he said, "Answer these questions, Dr. Ross."

Before he could start, I interjected, "You're worried, aren't you, that I'll ignore you during the Q&A session?"

"You're d--- right!" he shot back.

By now people were shouting, "Shut up!" or "Wait your turn, man!" I had a split second to pray and decide how to proceed. God answered.

"Let's let the professor ask his questions right now," I suggested, "and then he can decide whether to stay and hear more."

He smugly assumed I would be laughed off the stage when he asked a question about Noah's flood, then followed with, "How can you, a so-called scientist, believe in the utter nonsense of Genesis 1?" Of course, he was referring to particular interpretations of Genesis 1 and Genesis 6–8 that contradict the scientific record, and he assumed I would promote those views.

Instead, his questions gave me a welcomed opportunity to describe how my first reading of those passages had helped convince me the Bible must be true, given how closely it aligns with established and emerging scientific data. That congruence, I explained, arose out of applying the scientific method to interpretation of the biblical texts. He looked stunned. Then his demeanor changed.

He turned to the audience, introduced himself as a professor of engineering and an atheist. He said he had debated Christians publicly, but until now had never heard anything reasonable coming out of their mouths. He promised to sit quietly on two conditions: the first, that everyone would pay careful attention; the second, that I would meet with him privately. I agreed.

You can imagine how this response affected the audience. It affected me, too. I saw once again how God enjoys turning what's intended to destroy into something that builds up. The students stayed late into the evening, and local believers who had come to help enjoyed many a crucial conversation.

When I met privately with the professor, he told me about the frustration of his previous encounters with Christians. Not only had they rejected the scientific data, but also they had maligned his character and motives, calling him deceived and a deceiver. I told him I understood, having met with a similar response.

He could not understand why I didn't share his rage against them or why I'd be willing to forgive them. For the next two hours we discussed the character of Christ and the significance of what he accomplished, on our behalf, on the cross. I assured him God would provide the willingness and the power to forgive, if he would ask. "I'm not ready," he said.

> **God enjoys turning what's intended to destroy into something that builds up.**

We corresponded for several years after our meeting, and I always asked, "Are you ready yet?" He passed away without letting me know whether he had taken that step. But I can say that my encounter with this professor strengthened my resolve to use a scientifically credible creation model approach whenever addressing university audiences, an approach that invites critique and testing.

Nobel Laureates

When my colleague Fazale Rana and I presented our biblically based creation model at the University of Illinois, Nobel laureate Paul Lauterbur served as one of three faculty respondents. Neither he nor the other two disputed our scientific data or biblical interpretation connected with it. Instead, they went off topic, discussing their views on the philosophy of science. All three either stated or hinted they had not previously heard a credible scientific defense of the Bible or the Christian faith.

While in Houston to present the basics of our creation model at Rice University, I also had the privilege to speak at Second Baptist Church. One afternoon not long thereafter, a phone call came from Ben Young, one of the church's pastors. He told me a chemistry professor at Rice University, the winner of the Nobel Prize in chemistry, had begun attending church and asking him questions only a scientist could answer. Ben wanted to know if I'd come to Houston to help by meeting with Dr. Rick Smalley.

I suggested that a second outreach event at Rice would provide an organic opportunity for me to meet with Smalley. Ben agreed and went to work, connecting with other Rice faculty and the campus Christian clubs. Within a few months, the event came together.

I invited Rick to meet with me before my talk. He agreed and came with many astute questions on topics ranging from creation "days" to the transdimensional attributes of God, the transdimensional nature of the Trinity, human free will and divine predestination, the problem of evil, heaven and hell, how Jesus of Nazareth could pay the ransom price for all of humanity's sins in just 6–9 hours on the cross, and how Jesus's resurrected, physical body could pass through walls. On a more personal note, he asked how I could remain excited about ongoing research if the Bible, to which nothing can be added, represents the whole truth. My reply, we can never plumb the depths of either God's world or God's Word. The more we learn from the book of nature, the more we learn of him.

Rick seemed receptive to my answers, and as our meeting ended he asked for an outline of the lecture I was about to give. I handed him a copy as we headed to the auditorium. Rick took the only seat available, right in front of me in the second row. He sat close enough that I could see him taking copious notes throughout my talk as well as during the Q&A session afterward. I thought perhaps he planned to send me a detailed critique and additional questions.

A few weeks later I received an email from Rick. He said he had decided to do

We can never plumb the depths of either God's world or God's Word.

an experiment: he gave my lecture to a thousand students at Tuskegee University. To his astonishment, those students gave him a standing ovation. Based on that response to the content, he asked to read some of my books.

Through reading and in-depth conversations with fellow chemist James Tour, Pastor Ben Young, and others, Rick came to trust in Jesus Christ as his Creator and Savior. Once openly antagonistic to the Christian faith, he walked forward for baptism at Second Baptist Church. We stayed in touch until his untimely death from cancer. Just the day before he died he finished reading our book, *Who Was Adam?*,[1] and provided a wonderful endorsement of it. At Rick and his wife's request, I presented "reasons for hope" to his colleagues and a host of community and government leaders at his memorial service.[2]

Biology Professor

Rick had just a few years to share his faith among his peers and students at Rice, but I'm thankful for his boldness and for that of every faculty person who speaks openly about their faith in Jesus Christ. A biology professor at a San Francisco Bay Area college sets an encouraging example. He assisted Christian clubs on campus in arranging an outreach for me in the school's largest lecture hall. He also helped publicize my talk on scientific evidences for the God of the Bible.

In his introduction and closing remarks he told the audience that if anyone wanted to discuss science-and-faith topics or other "God questions" with him in the days after this event, they could sign up for appointments on a clipboard hanging outside his office door. A week later, he called me, laughing. "No one can tell me students aren't spiritually hungry," he said. "My appointment schedule is full till the end of the school year!" Many students came to faith on account of his readiness to give reasons for hope in Christ.

Chapter 10

Ready to Fly

Once upon a time, the glamour of travel included both the anticipated destination and the process of reaching it, especially if it involved a gleaming aircraft. My sons have difficulty believing that people once considered going to the airport and riding on an airplane a fun, exciting adventure. They can barely recall the days before TSA.

They also wonder how to explain, apart from supernatural intervention, why their dad—so reserved and nondescript—nearly always comes home with a unique souvenir, the tale of a highly improbable encounter either during a flight or while waiting for one. Working on my computer as I travel does seem to stack the odds in my favor, but many of these unlikely interactions occur even before I can open it. I'm convinced the explanation comes from Jesus's words about the Father's and his own ongoing Sabbath "work" (John 5:17).

Montreal Businessman

Any connection with hockey can spark a conversation on flights to or from Canada, and my father bequeathed me a good one. He designed and installed the glass shield at the former home of the Montreal Canadiens. That fact and a reference to Montreal as my birthplace made an easy conversation opener on a cross-country flight beside a Canadian businessman, a huge Canadiens fan.

This man started by telling me about his wonderful life. He painted a verbal portrait of his beautiful wife, his children now successfully launched in promising careers, a growing business of 25+ years with loyal employees and customers, his palatial home in Montreal, plus a lakeside vacation home with a boathouse and a couple of boats. He signed this picture with a flourish, saying "life is good."

I congratulated him on his achievements and asked him if he had a purpose in life, beyond making money and enjoying his leisure. Instantly the conversation and his countenance changed. After glancing out the window for a few moments, he revealed that his wife of thirty years had just complained to him that their relationship seemed hollow, devoid of meaning or purpose. She more than hinted at her readiness to leave him if he didn't develop, soon, some meaningful purpose for the rest of their lives together.

"I'm at a complete loss," he said, "on how to proceed. How can I satisfy my wife's request and save our marriage?" He then asked about my sense of purpose and whether I could offer him any advice.

What better opening can a person ask for? *God help me*, I prayed, *not to get so eager that I overwhelm this man with words*. I began by telling a little about my background and my initial belief that astronomy research would be my life's purpose. Then I described how my life's trajectory changed and why, bringing in some of the fine-tuning evidence I found so compelling (see chapter 2).

He wanted more evidence for God's existence and for God's purpose in creating the universe and humanity. He wanted to know God's plan for achieving that purpose, given the mess human beings are in. This question led to a discussion about Jesus and what he made possible for us. With a couple in the row behind us obviously leaning in, the Montreal businessman asked me to explain how he could receive forgiveness and a personal, purposeful relationship with God. In fact, he asked me to repeat my explanation because he wanted to share it with his wife. I did repeat it and then silently prayed that the Holy Spirit would move in his life, also in his wife, children, and employees, as well as in the lives of the eavesdropping couple.

Please Watch My Bags

For some reason, people waiting for flights often ask me, a total stranger, to please watch their luggage while they buy some food or use the restroom. I'm told I have a face people can trust. If at all possible, I agree to do it because when people return to recover their bags, they tend to ask where I'm headed and for what purpose.

Recently, one of these trusting souls asked if I had come to town to participate in the neuroscience conference there. I said, "No, I came for a different conference, one on the topic of creation and evolution." She introduced herself as a neuroscientist and said she took the evolution side. In her view, neuroscience could best be explained by humans' and great apes' descent from a relatively recent common ancestor.

"But I do believe in God," she added, and went on to identify herself as a universalist—one who thinks God saves everyone, regardless of what they believe about Jesus Christ.

I commented that I take a different perspective on both science and salvation, and to my surprise she began to ask questions. First she wanted to know what I believe about human origins, and then she asked about Earth's first life. When I mentioned my colleagues' research and my having coauthored books on these topics, she pulled out a pen and made note of the titles, as well as the Reasons to Believe web address.

She then asked me why I believe salvation comes only through making Jesus Christ the master of one's life and accepting his offer of forgiveness. In particular, the concept of grace intrigued her, as did my statement about the inadequacy of "good works" to satisfy God's righteous standard. She listened intently as I explained what I've learned from the Bible on these subjects. As I got up to board my flight, I noticed that she had already begun perusing reasons.org. "Let me know if you have more questions," I said, and she replied, "I will."

Engineer and Neuropsychologist

The airplane I boarded after saying goodbye to the neuroscientist was a relatively small one, with engines near the back. My aisle seat near the front looked like a good place to get some work done. So I pulled out my computer and popped it open. What appeared on my screen I don't recall, but whatever it was it caught the attention of the man across the aisle from me.

Science makes sense only if God is simultaneously one essence and three distinct persons.

He introduced himself as an engineer. "I'd like to believe in God," he began, "but I'm the kind of guy who needs facts." He wanted to know if I could give him any solid scientific evidence for the existence of God.

I started with evidence from big bang cosmology, then went on to cite the origin of Earth's first life, the origin of human beings, and the fine-tuning of not only the universe, but also of the Milky Way Galaxy, our solar system, and Earth to make humans and human civilization possible. He seemed to take it all in, but then he wanted to know why I had concluded that this Creator could only be the God of the Bible.

I pointed out that only the Bible reveals God as a triune Being—three persons and one essence, at the same time. We talked about transdimensionality and why science makes sense only if God is simultaneously one essence and three distinct persons, all three manifesting identical character attributes, sharing identical plans and purposes, feeling and expressing the same emotions, and always agreeing on their decisions. He thanked me profusely for the conversation and for the evidence I had given him. He asked for my business card and made a few notes on the back of it.

The young man in the window seat beside me spoke up then, saying he had enjoyed overhearing my conversation with the engineer. He asked me to repeat in more detail my thoughts on why science makes sense only if God is a triune Being, and he listened intently. Soon I learned he had attended the same neuroscience conference as the woman I had met in the waiting area. He was about to take up a teaching position at Brigham Young University (BYU). We then spent about fifteen minutes or more discussing the differences between Mormonism and Christianity.

As our flight neared its end, he asked if I would be willing to give a lecture at BYU on the fine-tuning of the universe and what that fine-tuning implied about God. I let him know the BYU physics faculty had invited me once, but the theology department had canceled my invitation. "Would you mind if I were to try again?" he asked. I told him to go right ahead, and as the plane touched down we exchanged business cards.

Please Watch My Children

One afternoon during a three-hour layover in the Denver airport, a young woman with four little ones in tow interrupted my book writing to ask if I'd please look after her luggage—and her children—so she could "take care of some things." She seemed desperate, and the kids looked well-behaved. So, of course, I agreed.

I entertained the kids by showing them some of the nature photos on my computer, especially the animal shots I've collected on my adventures in the Canadian mountains. They also enjoyed the video clip of a dancing, screeching cockatoo I sometimes use in one of my talks. About a half hour later, the mom returned.

She apologized for interrupting me and taking so long. "Somehow I knew my kids would be safe with you," she said, and then asked what I was working on.

As I described the book in progress, she began to ask questions. I learned that science or, rather, her misconceptions about it had been keeping her away from belief in God. She wanted to know if I had already published anything on science, the Bible, and Christianity. As I extended a business card, she snatched it with a smile and a thank-you and ran with her children to catch their connecting flight.

Quantum Physicist

On another occasion, as I waited to board a packed flight to Seattle, the loudspeaker squawked out my name. Knowing I held the cheapest of tickets, I dreaded news that I'd been bumped. Instead, the desk staff asked if I was traveling alone. I said, "Yes." They told me a young family on this flight had requested to sit together and asked if I would mind changing seats. I said, "No problem. Seat me anywhere you need to." The attendant then handed me my new boarding pass. It read seat 2B, in the first-class section!

A tall man with a thick German accent settled into 2A, wearing a look as pleased as I felt. "I never fly first class," he said, "but Microsoft bought my ticket."

I asked if he worked for Microsoft. "Only as a consultant," he replied. Then, without further small talk, he introduced himself as a quantum physicist and an atheist. When he learned my identity, a Canadian astrophysicist and a Christian, he said, "This is going to be an interesting flight."

After takeoff the questions began, one after another. "If your Christian God wanted humans," he challenged, "why would the universe be so vast?" Then, "Why would it be so old?" Then, "Why so dark?" and "Why so entropic?" Over the course of two hours, we discussed why the universe had to be exactly as it is to make even one planet capable of hosting billions of humans at one time. He expressed special interest in why the laws of physics would be as they are, intrigued by my claim of a connection between them and the restraint of evil.

"I have one more question," the man said as our flight neared its end. "How is it that you have these well-prepared answers to all my questions?"

I told him so many people, both scientists and nonscientists, wonder about these same questions that I had written a book about them. When I pulled a copy of *Why the Universe Is the Way It Is* out of my briefcase, he seemed incredulous. But, then he turned to the table of contents. All his questions appeared there as chapter titles.

He stared at the book, wide-eyed for a moment, and I asked if he'd like to keep it. He nodded, then asked if I had produced any material in German. One DVD remained in my bag, *Journey toward Creation*, the multilingual version,

German included.

As the two of us walked toward baggage claim, together we calculated the odds of a Canadian-born Christian astrophysicist sitting beside a German atheist quantum physicist in the first-class cabin of a US flight between San Francisco and Seattle. Less than one chance in a billion, we figured. With that we concluded, "Our meeting was no accident."

Ken's Story

The story of my interaction with the quantum physicist and others like it stirred a reaction in my colleague, Ken Samples, similar to that of my class member, Jackie Stewart, years earlier. Here, Ken tells in his own words, how God dealt with his skepticism:

I have known Hugh Ross for over twenty years and have worked closely with him at the science-faith apologetics organization he founded, Reasons to Believe (RTB). For years I had heard Hugh talk about his many evangelistic and apologetics encounters with people when traveling to and from his speaking events. Because he described so many rather dramatic encounters with people, especially at airports and on airplanes, I began to wonder if he might be embellishing aspects of these stories. After all, he reported these stories at staff meetings where I thought he may be trying to inspire all of us in our pursuit of the Great Commission (reaching the world with the message of salvation through Jesus Christ).

I should also note that as a philosopher I tend to be a rather critical thinker, generally questioning the things I hear even from someone as trustworthy as Hugh. Adopting a healthy dose of skepticism was part of my philosophical training. However, an experience or two while traveling with Hugh ended my skeptical concerns about his stories.

As I traveled with Hugh to a series of outreach events, we had a layover at the Portland International Airport. Sitting together in a crowded section of the airport waiting for our next flight, Hugh made a call on his cell phone to his wife, Kathy, to discuss the editing of a new edition of his booklet, Genesis One: A Scientific Perspective.

During the conversation Hugh specifically talked about the creation days in the first chapter of Genesis and how they aligned with scientific thinking. I noticed during this call that a man sitting about ten feet away from us had leaned toward us and appeared to be listening intently to Hugh's comments. Sure enough, when Hugh ended his call, the man came over to us and immediately began raising questions about the Bible and modern science. The three of us talked for some time about various science-faith issues. While the man remained somewhat skeptical concerning the Bible and Christianity overall, he was nevertheless cordial and seemed deeply interested in our perspective on science-faith issues. As our plane arrived for boarding, we shook hands with him and exchanged business cards.

However, that wasn't the end of our encounter with this thoughtful individual, a professor of computer science at Stanford University, according to his card. During our flight he left his seat in the first-class section and walked to the back of the plane where Hugh and I were seated, to an empty seat beside us, and continued our discussion. This robust dialogue concerning science and faith continued until the flight attendant asked him to return to his seat for the plane's landing. I was truly amazed at the interest this Stanford scholar showed in dialoguing with us about the Bible. This evangelistic-apologetics encounter reminded me of the apostle Paul's encounters in the book of Acts.

Hugh always emphasizes that if Christians are prepared to share their faith, then God will orchestrate opportunities. Another experience drove this truth home to me, personally.

I was standing in the Dallas/Fort Worth International Airport waiting to board my flight when a man walked up to me and began a conversation. I was tired and trying to focus on getting in the appropriate line to board the plane. So, I was minimally responsive to the man's attempt to talk with me. But this man was intent on doing so. When he asked me what I did for a living, I thought, If I tell him I'm a Christian apologist he'll immediately lose interest in talking with me. *I was wrong.* When I told him that I lectured and wrote books in the field of Christian apologetics, he smiled and shared with me that two of his favorite Christian apologetics writers were Walter Martin and Hugh Ross.

If Christians are prepared to share their faith, then God will orchestrate opportunities.

When I revealed that I had worked for Martin at the Christian Research Institute (CRI) and currently worked for Ross at RTB, he then added that he was familiar with my apologetics work, as well. I learned that this man was a dentist and a member of the Seventh-day Adventist Church. During our flight, he found a seat *near me and we discussed theological issues the whole way. I later wondered about the probability that I would bump into a man who knew the names of my two bosses, Walter Martin and Hugh Ross. I became firmly convinced that Hugh is right about God providentially orchestrating encounters amid travel.*

Seminary Professor and Pastor

Although many or most of my memorable travel encounters involve interaction with nonbelievers, God sometimes brings me into contact with a fellow Christian, too, or someone who self-identifies as a Christian. I am amazed, though I shouldn't be, how often God connects me with Christian leaders who struggle with science-faith issues.

On a recent cross-country flight, the woman seated next to me held a dual appointment as a seminary professor and a pastor. When I asked her what perspective she takes on the Bible, she said she views it as a book of "inspiration and wisdom on how we should relate to one another and take care of the environment." She added that much of her teaching was devoted to helping students and parishioners understand that the Bible is valuable, but not inerrant. The toughest aspect of her job, she sighed, was debating with fundamentalists who actually insist that the Bible is scientifically and historically accurate.

I asked where she thought the Bible was mistaken in its statements about nature and history. She immediately cited the Genesis account of creation and the story of Noah's flood. She said a thousand years ago Christians might have believed such things, but today's scientists had thoroughly refuted them. Today we know, she added, that a global flood never occurred and the order of creation events in Genesis 1 is all wrong.

This seemed a good moment to ask if she or any of her seminary colleagues had ever met a scientist who considered the Bible inerrant. She said I must be referring to young-earth creationists. "The problem with those people," she declared, "is that the scientific community and the Supreme Court have exposed their so-called science as completely lacking in credibility."

"Have you ever met any *other* scientists who take an inerrant view of Scripture?" I queried.

"No," she replied, "and I doubt such a scientist exists."

When I let her know she had just now met one, she stifled a gasp. Then she politely questioned my credentials. She showed surprise to hear I'd done research at Caltech and knew other Christians there. She expressed even more astonishment when I mentioned having lectured at a dozen seminaries or more in North America and abroad.

Before long she began to ask questions, starting with one about how a credible scientist could possibly consider Genesis 1 a plausible narrative. As you can imagine from what you know of my story, a lengthy discussion ensued. Our topics ranged from the scientific method, rooted in Scripture, and how it makes sense of the sequence of creation events to the purpose, extent, and timing of the "worldwide," not global, flood. We talked about the many biblical forecasts of later discoveries in biology, medicine, physics, astronomy, and other disciplines, including some of the most recent findings.

She seemed intrigued but expressed her hesitancy to accept my words, given that in all her studies she'd never come across other scholars, whether scientists or theologians, who held views similar to mine. I mentioned a few historical figures and then asked if she knew of theologian and biblical scholar Gleason Archer. This name and reputation seemed somewhat familiar to her. So, I described my dialogue with him and other professors during a lecture series I'd presented at Trinity Evangelical Divinity School (TEDS). Over lunch with a group of TEDS professors and me, he shared with some glee that in 1955 his exegetical study of Genesis 1 had led to an interpretation identical to mine. When colleagues asked, "Why didn't you publish it?" he replied, "I didn't have the scientific knowledge to back it up."

From this point our discussion turned to the "higher criticism" on which her theological training rested. She allowed me to challenge some of its assumptions, and though the dialogue at moments became intense, it remained friendly. As the flight neared its end, I asked if she'd be interested in a book on the topics we'd discussed. She seemed amazed that I had one and graciously accepted it, along with my business card. At this point, the couple seated behind us piped up.

"Could we have your card, too?" they asked. "We really enjoyed your conversation, and we'd like to ask a couple of questions, too."

Discouraged Pastor

With only 0.2 percent of the American population employed as pastors,[1] I find it hard to consider my many meetings with pastors in airports and on airplanes as random encounters.[2] Sometimes God works through these pastors to encourage me, and other times he allows me to uplift them. Either way, we both walk away glad to have met.

I may not be adept at reading body language, but even I noticed that the man seated beside me on an airplane seemed downhearted. Not sure he'd be open to talking, I thought I'd at least tell him my name and ask his. He told me his name, John, and said he pastored a church, "for now." His tone suggested "not for much longer." Then he began pouring out his heart.

He let me know he had been thoroughly humiliated by some of the most brilliant members of his congregation. They pressed him to back away from his naive and backward notions about creation and evolution and Old Testament miracle stories because well-established scientific facts contradict them. It's okay to teach about Christ, they said, but he'd never reach intelligent, educated people if he kept insisting the Bible had anything to say about natural history, in particular.

These words and the confident condescension behind them had shaken Pastor John to the core, he said, and he could see the effect on his preaching. "I know my congregation can tell I'm intimidated," he confided. "Many people have already left." He went on to confess his deeper anguish: "I'm not even sure I believe the Bible anymore, or that my faith is real."

That's a difficult place for a pastor to be, I acknowledged. He nodded and then began to ask questions about what I do for a living. I'd love to have a video of the slow-motion change in Pastor John's demeanor. Words cannot adequately capture it. After finding his voice, he began to pepper me, rapid fire, with questions.

During the next 90 minutes, at his request, I summarized the content of a dozen or so books addressing reasons to believe that the Bible is totally true and trustworthy, no matter what topic it addresses. He seemed especially overjoyed to hear that I knew many scientists, some professors at revered secular universities, who share my convictions and commit time to personal outreach among students and peers. I let him know, also, that he'd be more than welcome to participate in a Reasons to Believe chapter that meets in his city. Together we agreed, "God put us together today!"

National Church Leader

If finding myself beside a pastor no longer surprises me, meeting a leader of the National Council of Churches (NCC) in the next seat certainly does. The distinguished gentleman in my row on a cross-country flight also held a seminary professorship. He seemed equally surprised to find himself next to a scientist-turned-pastor. Apparently, I was the first of that kind he had met.

The passion he expressed for helping Americans and Westerners, in general, become more biblically literate gave us a point of agreement. He described various ideas for making the Bible available, as a whole or in parts, in as many media formats as possible. No doubt he applauds, as I do, the opening of the

Museum of the Bible in Washington, DC.

Although his position on Scripture differed from mine and resembled that of other seminarians I've met, including those of the woman I'd met on a previous flight, he did invite me to explain how a scientist would make a case for biblical inerrancy. He gave no indication of readiness to change his view. However, after our two-hour conversation, he did acknowledge that my view represented an academically viable interpretive option, one that warranted consideration. He encouraged me to seize any and all media opportunities that might come to my ministry team and me. If we could create some of our own, all the better, he said.

Once again, God used an encounter to benefit me, and to affirm the value of respectful dialogue with Christians whose views collide with our own. Just as importantly, he reminded me that the outcome of any conversation belongs to him. We may not see that our interaction had any impact at all, but more often than not, we serve as soil tenders, seed planters, weeders, and waterers. Some day, when the Lord harvests his crop for eternal life, "the sower and the reaper may be glad together" (John 4:36).

Uber Encounter

With my sons no longer available to transport me to and from local airports, God has provided a new means of connecting me with spiritually hungry people. Perhaps you've discovered it, too. If not, I hope you soon will.

When Uber driver Marco picked me up for an early morning ride to LAX (Los Angeles International Airport), he warned me that traffic looked even worse than usual. His app showed heavy congestion not only on the way but especially in the loop leading from terminal to terminal inside. I suggested he drop me off outside of the airport, if that would save him a hassle.

> **We may not see that our interaction had any impact at all, but more often than not, we serve as soil tenders.**

Marco replied, "No one worries about *my* time. Who are you, anyway?" Taken aback for a moment, I gave him my name, and before I could say more he asked where I was headed and what for, work or pleasure.

"Virginia, and for both," I told him, and then explained I'd be speaking on science and faith, something I greatly enjoyed.

"I always thought science disproves God," Marco commented. "And just so you know, I'm not religious."

"I'm not religious either," I said.

"Mind if I ask you some questions?" he asked.

You can guess my answer. Before asking anything, Marco told me his mother had taken him to a Catholic church when he was a child, but no one there would answer his questions. He said he couldn't understand things like how Jesus could be God if the Father is also God and why, if there's a good God, he allows so much pain and suffering.

I silently thanked God for the slow traffic and began to tackle Marco's questions, letting him know he could interrupt me any time if what I said seemed unclear. We started with his assumption that science undermines belief in God. I gave him an abbreviated version of my story, and he listened intently. We talked about God's transcendence as the answer to mysteries such as God's three-ness and oneness, human freedom and God's sovereignty, Jesus's humanity and deity. Then I explained how the Bible alone makes sense of the world's pain and suffering and shows us the way to a life of meaning and purpose. Marco asked me to explain that last part slowly and clearly because he wanted to remember it. He insisted on taking me through the LAX loop to my terminal, "for my sake," he said. He even tried to refuse payment for our one-hour-and-forty-minute ride. Never had I felt more grateful for LA traffic.

As we parted, he shook my hand firmly and thanked me again and again. He pocketed my card and started to get back into his car. Then he jumped back out again to ask, "Which of your books should I read first?"

Though my flight hadn't yet left the ground, I felt as if my trip had already proved wholly worthwhile.

Chapter 11

Always Means *Always*

The growing ubiquity of digital devices means fewer opportunities for conversation, in the air or just about anywhere else. Once the ear buds go in, talking goes out. To be honest, I sometimes look forward to a long, quiet flight as a time to catch up on some writing or to update a Keynote presentation, especially if my preparation time has been crunched. And yet, I've learned not to count on it. Peter's reminder to "set Christ apart as Lord in your hearts" (NET) means Christ's plan for my day and my time trumps my plan, even if my plan seems a really good and important one. When he says "always" be ready, he adds no "unless . . ."

Midair Outreach

On the way to a conference in the Midwest, where I'd be addressing Christians who hold diverse positions on the meaning of Genesis 1, I felt relieved to see the young man next to me grab a pillow, pop in earplugs, and settle for a nap. My talk needed more polishing, and now I'd have time to work on it. So, as soon as the plane leveled off after takeoff, I whipped out my Mac and pulled up my presentation slides.

Christ's plan for my day and my time trumps my plan.

After a short time, the refreshment cart rumbled by my aisle seat and the attendant propelling it took my request for an orange juice, no ice. When she handed it over, her eyes fell on my screen and widened. She motioned to another attendant, whispered, "Cover for me," and knelt down beside me.

"Do you mind if I ask you some questions?" she said, softly. "I'm *very* interested in what you're working on."

She stayed with me for half the flight, wanting to see and ask questions about each slide of my talk. Our conversation attracted the attention of a geologist seated a couple rows back. He and two others joined the flight attendant in the aisle, bringing their own questions. Meanwhile, the couple in the row behind me bent over the seat to listen in.

Our little gathering began to break up when the flight attendant realized the need to return to her duties, but her return freed another attendant to come by with her questions. Before that flight ended, at least seven people heard scientific evidence for the reliability of the biblical creation account. And, if I wanted a chance to hone my conference talks, God provided it in a way I could not have anticipated.

This story brings to mind another midair, unscheduled outreach event. It started at the back of a smaller, 72-seat aircraft. Again seated comfortably on the aisle, I relished the opportunity to review my message on "Cosmic Reasons to Believe in Jesus Christ." Two gentlemen across the aisle noticed my slides and wanted to know what I was working on. One commented, "It looks more interesting than this book I brought."

Not wanting to disturb the peace of other passengers, I tried to keep my voice low, but apparently it carried. My answers to the men's questions drew others to the back of the plane. When a flight attendant strode rapidly toward us, I thought, *uh-oh*, and assumed this impromptu gathering would come to an abrupt end. Instead, to my amazement, the gracious attendant reorganized the seating arrangement so that a dozen people, including her, could see my slides and hear my talk.

Skeptics Society

Exhausted. Drained. That's how I felt after two days at ORIGINS, the BIG Questions, an international conference sponsored by the Skeptics Society and held at Caltech. Five lectures from several of the world's leading atheist and agnostic scientists covered their scientific reasons for concluding that the God of the Bible does not exist. The conference culminated with a debate between particle physicist and professor of philosophical atheism Victor Stenger and me on the subject, Great God Debate: Does Science Support Belief in a Deity?

Rather than focus on the content of that debate or on Stenger's bold closing comment (a video recording is available for those who are curious[1]) I would like to describe the reaction of the 700+ skeptics in the audience.

During the first part of the formal Q&A session, nearly all the questions were directed to me. Eventually the executive director of the Skeptics Society,

Michael Shermer, stepped on stage to announce that the remainder of the questions must be posed to Stenger and the other conference speakers.

Shermer's announcement seemed to frustrate many in the audience. So, I stayed for an additional three hours to answer questions and engage in conversation. Nearly everyone who approached greeted me warmly. I cannot count the number of people who said they had never heard a credible scientific defense of the Bible and the Christian faith before. They had assumed no such defense existed. They described Christians' response to the subject of science and faith as one of silence, panic, a quick change of the subject, or a litany of scientific nonsense.

This response, they said, had led them to conclude that atheists and agnostics "own science." Some acknowledged I had given them cause to doubt their conclusion. I said I valued their honesty.

As I was about to head to my car, a cluster of about thirty people crowded around me. They wanted to know if my experience at their conference had changed any of my views. I said, "Yes. This event actually strengthened my faith in the God of the Bible."

"How?" they asked.

I told them I couldn't help but notice that only the God of the Bible had been singled out for attention, and I could see only one reason for the degree of passion aimed toward this supposedly nonexistent deity.

"What's that?" they asked. I said, "If you really were convinced that the God of the Bible doesn't exist, you'd treat him as you do the Easter bunny or the tooth fairy. But your fixation and emotion say something else. I think you really do believe the God of the Bible exists, but you don't like him."

One of them spoke for the whole group, "I see what you're getting at. It's not so much that we hate the God of the Bible, but we despise his followers." Then, various members of the group began to relate hurtful encounters with, or mistreatment by people who identified themselves as evangelical Christians.

I told them I was sad and sorry to hear of these experiences, but I also appealed to these logic-based engineers and scientists to consider the illogic of allowing poorly behaved humans, creatures prone to lie, cheat, and abuse, to come between them and a transcendent God who never lies, never cheats, never abuses, never fails, always loves, and eagerly communicates truth.

After a brief silence, several acknowledged the validity of my point. Then they challenged me to use whatever influence I may have in the Christian community to encourage believers to behave at least as charitably toward them as they had behaved toward me. I said I would, and this book is part of my attempt to fulfill that promise.

Atheist in a Coma

When a nurse friend, Jeannine, called me about one of her patients, nearly everyone around her assumed the time for a pastoral visit had passed. The patient, a former Caltech physicist, had already slipped into a coma, and no one expected him to hang onto life for more than a day or two. He and his family were not believers, but Jeannine couldn't shake the impression that he might respond positively to hearing about Christ from another physicist. So I came.

> **Consider the illogic of allowing poorly behaved humans . . . to come between them and a transcendent God.**

The man's wife stood at the foot of the bed and his daughter, beside him, holding his hand. I told the wife I'd done research on galaxies at Caltech and had heard her husband was also a Caltech researcher. She nodded.

"I'm also a pastor," I said, "and I'd like to talk to your husband about the transition from this life to the next."

"No," she snapped, "you may *not*. My husband and I are atheists, and even if he were able to hear anything at this point, he'd be highly offended by any talk about God."

"Before you give me an absolute *no*," I appealed, "let me share with you what I'd hoped to say to your husband. Then, if you find my words are offensive, I'll leave and not bother you further." Before she could object, I began speaking loudly enough that if the man still had any auditory capacity, he could hear.

As I began to explain the gospel basics, the daughter exclaimed, "He's squeezing my hand, Mother!" Not sure how to interpret the squeeze, I kept going. A minute later, the daughter said, "He's squeezing harder."

"You must be mistaken," said the wife.

I continued, and when I got to the part about repentance and receiving God's forgiveness for sin, past, present, and future, the daughter announced, "He opened his eyes!"

The wife insisted he could not have, and because I was causing a disturbance, I must leave immediately. On my way out, I heard the daughter say, "He really did open them."

The next day, when alone with her patient, Jeannine repeated my words, "just in case." She told me stress lines had left the man's face, and he visibly relaxed as she spoke. Two days later, the physicist passed into eternity.

Late Night Grocery Run

The hour was late, after 11 PM, as Kathy and I headed home from a meeting, tired and looking forward to sleep. Suddenly, Kathy announced that we needed to stop at the grocery store. None of the two or three items she listed seemed all that critical to me. I *really* wanted to go straight home and suggested waiting till tomorrow. But, for some inexplicable reason, this stop could not wait.

Baffled and slightly irritated, I got out of the car and trudged into the market to retrieve the items for her. I picked them up as quickly as I could and was hustling toward the checkout when a loud cry echoed through the all-but-empty store. "It's you! It's you!" I turned toward the voice and spotted a woman from our Bible study group.

Lana walked toward me, bursting into sobs. As soon as she could speak, she poured out her story. She told me she and her husband had been struggling to keep their marriage together but putting up a good front at the study, not wanting anyone to know. Recently, their conflicts had escalated to a point she could no longer tolerate. Just hours ago, after another painful clash, she had told him, "I'm done!" She threw some clothes, shoes, and a few other essentials into her car and sped off. Then she realized she'd forgotten to grab some food for her flight. So, she stopped at the store on her way.

"As soon as I saw you," she said, "I knew I was rebelling against God by running away." At that very moment Lana repented. She admitted she needed God's help to return home and begin the hard work of restoring her marriage—no more hiding or pretending. I assured her that help was available and she'd have the support of our whole group. She relaxed and nodded.

I paid the cashier while Lana reshelved the cereal box and other items she'd picked up. As we exited the store, she paused to ask, "Why are *you* here at this hour, anyway?"

When I told her, she insisted on walking to the car with me. Kathy, who'd nearly fallen asleep while waiting, looked up with a start to see Lana beside her window. Lana signaled for her to roll it down. "I want you to know God used you tonight," she said, "to stop me from making a disastrous mistake." She added, "Nothing less than seeing Hugh in this store could have kept me from leaving my husband."

Lana did return to her husband. They did seek help from a marriage counselor. Their restored relationship grew and strengthened with every passing year and became a source of help to many others.

God had a message for me that night, too. His guidance may not always align with my convenience or common sense. I need to consider, always, that God directs my path, just as he guided the Sun, Moon, and stars into place.

Pornographers' Interview

My staff expressed shock when the producer of a popular radio talk show called to request an interview with me on the program. The topic, he said, would be evidence for God. I agreed to the interview, not knowing that, in this case, "talk" really meant "shock."

> **God directs my path, just as he guided the Sun, Moon, and stars into place.**

The studio address took me to an unfamiliar part of downtown Los Angeles. An armed guard appeared as I drove up. He directed me to park inside the barbed wire enclosed lot. "The hosts are already on the air," he said, "so go sit in the green room. They'll call you when they're ready."

The so-called green room featured two uncomfortable chairs, no table, dim lighting, and walls plastered with obscene posters. In one corner stood a life-sized cutout of a naked Howard Stern, making me grateful for the lack of light. Two speakers blared the on-air dialogue with the four hosts and callers to the show.

I had no choice but to listen, figuring I'd at least be a little better prepared for my interview. Soon it became even clearer that these guys were deeply into pornography. One bragged to a caller about the quality of the latest hardcore film he had produced. Their words I cannot and would not quote, but their attitude toward women and morality repelled me.

After about fifteen minutes I walked into the hallway to see if I could find someone to turn off, or at least turn down, the sound in that room. Alas, I was met with locked doors and no answers to my knocking. Back I went to the torture chamber.

This time I stuffed my ears with tissue, pulled out my computer, and tried to focus on my writing. The tissue barely blunted the sound, but I kept plugging away.

Roughly an hour passed before the green room door opened. The show's producer looked surprised to see me still there. With a laugh he told me, "You're the first Christian who's survived the green room test, man. You'll be the first Christian we've ever interviewed."

Once situated in the studio, I met the four hosts, young men in their late twenties or early thirties. Their first question on the air, "So, what do you think of our show?"

"It seems to me you're trying too hard," I replied, "to make your show as raunchy as possible." I added, "From hearing bits and pieces of your conversation, I'd say you're all more intelligent and better educated than you let on." Faces and postures shifted.

"Let's get to your thoughts on what we said last hour about the Bible and Christians."

I said I'd have to agree with some of their critique *IF* what they criticized reflected what the Bible actually taught, but it didn't. "What you said about scientific nonsense in the Bible is patently false. You're picking on one narrow view of what it says, not on the words themselves."

For the next half hour, they listened, rarely interrupting, as I described how the biblical text matched up with the scientific record and gave rise to the advance of science. Next, they asked how I became a Christian. They seemed astounded to learn that science, not a family member or friend, persuaded me that the Bible is the Word of God. They wanted the details.

One of the four confessed he did believe in God, but he never knew why. The other three said they'd like to believe, but that they had too many unanswered questions. For the rest of the show I fielded their questions about the Trinity, the problem of evil, evolution and the origin of life, other world religions, people who've "never heard," and more. For 90 minutes, the call-in lines blinked, but no calls were taken.

During commercial breaks, the producer made cracks about how the language had changed. Two of the hosts kept eyeing two of the books I'd brought with me. "Would you like these?" I asked. "They're yours if you'll read them." Each took one. Then the guard escorted me out.

All the way home, I prayed. Back at the office I enlisted others to pray. I could only cling to God's promise in Isaiah 55:11, saying, "[My word] will not return to me empty, but will accomplish what I desire and achieve the purpose for which I sent it."

Skid Row

Many years ago, my wife, Kathy, and I had to run an errand in downtown Los Angeles. Parking in downtown Los Angeles is a challenge, to say the least. We had to park our car several blocks away from our destination in the middle of Skid Row.

On the way back to our car, we walked toward an obviously homeless man approximately in his late fifties. We thought he was going to panhandle us. He looked at us and said, "I don't want your money." I replied, "Then, why are you on the street here?"

The man asked us if we really wanted to know. Something in our spirit told us we needed to put our schedule aside and listen to this man. Our willingness to listen caused the man to open up about his life in ways that surprised us both.

As the man began to tell his tale of woe and complain about our nation's political and judicial systems, we noted that his vocabulary, diction, and grammar were exceptional. I said to him, "Sir, you seem to be highly educated." His response, "How would you know?" When he found out about our degrees and the occupations we held, he told us his whole story.

He said he was a surgeon and that he was so successful in his surgeries that he was made the chief of surgery for a major hospital. In that role, however, the hospital put demands on him that he insisted no human could possibly fulfill. When he appealed to the hospital administrators for a measure of relief, he stated to us that they flatly refused to offer any and, eventually, refused to even listen to him. Meanwhile, his wife sued for divorce. In the midst of divorce proceedings, he found himself named as a codefendant in a medical malpractice suit. He said the stress was so great in his life and the threat of impending crushing debt so enormous that he had no other option but to chuck everything and live out the rest of his days homeless and invisible on the streets of Los Angeles.

I gently pointed out that he seemed to be bitter about the way his life turned out. He replied that we would be just as bitter as he if we had suffered a fate similar to his. We asked if he had considered that perhaps the bitterness he had harbored years ago may have brought on some of the relationship difficulties he experienced. He said he would need to think about that.

What gave us hope for this man is that he openly acknowledged that he was bitter and was unable to forgive certain individuals who wronged him. What gave us some reasons to despair, however, was that we were not certain he was responding positively to our exhortations that he go to God for the forgiveness that he lacked and that he humble himself before God in admitting that it was wrong to harbor all the bitterness that he held. We left him with a promise: God would take away his bitterness if he would let him.

That day we could have ignored the man's statement, "I don't want your money," and continued on our way to our car. The Spirit of God within us would not let that happen. The voice of God in our spirit powerfully compelled us to put aside that day's to-do list and respond.

We don't know what happened to that man on Skid Row. We do not even know how true his story was. We do know, though, that God spoke to us to plant a seed of hope in a man who, at that time, seemed completely bereft of hope.

Bank Outreach

Scotsmen have a well-earned reputation for thriftiness, and my Highlander lineage seems evident in me. I hate waste, whether time or money or other resources. Thus, whenever I anticipate a long wait in line, I take work along with me. Why let precious minutes evaporate?

On one afternoon's trip to the bank, I perused my latest issue of the *Astrophysical Journal*, a hefty volume resembling an old-time metropolitan phone book. In a moment of boredom, the man behind me peered over my shoulder, then asked rather loudly, "What on earth are you reading?" I answered, and then came his next question, "Why?"

I began to explain how each volume of this journal provides additional evidence for the Creator and his fine-tuning of the cosmos for humanity's sake and for the fulfillment of his grand redemptive plan. By now the people in front of me had turned around and tuned in. As I filled in a few more details, one of the branch officers left her desk to listen in.

When the security guard scowled and took a step in our direction, I pulled a batch of business cards from my pocket and offered them to anyone who wanted one. Nine or ten people took one. So ended my first, but not my only, waiting-line outreach. Whether at a bank, supermarket, home improvement store, doctor's office, or (especially) the Department of Motor Vehicles, I never stand in line without something to work on, just in case, and just in case God has a different type of work in mind for me.

Bypass Surgery

Speaking at a conference for chaplains, I shared how science can be used to spark spiritual interest and confident faith in the hearts of the patients, police officers, military personnel, prisoners, and athletes—whomever these chaplains may serve. Especially in times of distress and danger, I said, people need evidence that God exists, that he shaped the universe and the world for a good purpose, that he knows and cares for each person, and that the Bible proves true and trustworthy in everything it communicates, including science and history.

Over lunch, some of the chaplains bemoaned the fact that many of their peers don't really believe what I said. Many don't even know the source of the hope and courage they attempt to provide. "Too bad they won't come to these trainings," one woman said. I told the group to let me know if I could help in any way and reminded them Reasons to Believe has books and videos and a website they could possibly share. Little did I know I'd be seeing one of them again very soon.

> **Especially in times of distress and danger . . . people need evidence that God exists.**

My friends joke that I'm "scary healthy." I exercise and eat right. My weight and blood test numbers even my doctor calls "enviable." But, on the last stiff hike of a wonderful vacation, a solo jaunt to capture another waterfall photo, I returned to Kathy looking unusually pale and winded.

On the two-day drive home, I felt fine, rested, and ready to jump back into my routine. The next morning's run suggested otherwise. I came back to the house with tightness in my chest and mild pain in my arms. Urged by Kathy and my friend Mark, I agreed to visit the nearest emergency room. The next morning I passed the stress test with flying colors and called Kathy to pick me up. She resisted when she learned no angiogram had been ordered, but the doctor signed me out and that was that.

However, Kathy couldn't let it go. She said, "I know something's wrong. You *need* that test."

I couldn't schedule it right away because of a speaking commitment in Toronto. Kathy wanted me to cancel but I promised to take it easy and back off from hard exercise. Again, I returned home feeling fine, but since the test had been booked and Kathy seemed so insistent, I went ahead with it.

To everyone's shock, the angiogram showed a near total blockage in an artery referred to as "the widow-maker." Because of its location, a stent would not do. The staff called for a cardiovascular surgeon. None was available on short notice at the small community hospital where I had the angiogram. So, the staff called for a doctor (a heart transplant specialist, as it turns out) from the Los Angeles County + University of Southern California Medical Center. Later that evening he performed single bypass surgery on me.

When Kathy came into the recovery room, one of the nurses backed up the surgeon's assurances that the surgery had gone quickly and well. Then the nurse said, "Just so you know, Mrs. Ross, one of the staff recognized your husband's name, and we already have a line of people waiting to talk with him."

Sure enough, after getting a little rest and coming back to check on me, tubes and wires still attached, Kathy found me already engaged in conversations about science and faith. For the next four days, I spent nearly all my waking hours answering questions, not just for various clinicians. Five different chaplains came to see me, and they brought questions, too.

The first four chaplains who visited me approached the Bible as "inspired," like poetry and art, they said, but not totally true. When I asked why, they asserted that science had exposed multiple errors in the Bible. I can't recall all the topics covered during those chaplain visits, but I do recall questions about the big bang, the first eleven chapters of Genesis, Adam and Eve, human exceptionalism, the image of God, the fossil record, and creation texts in Job, Psalms, and elsewhere in Scripture. Before leaving my room, each one asked what books my colleagues and I had written and wrote down our web address.

Meanwhile, my roommate had little choice but to hear all these conversations. Weak and barely able to speak, he never participated in them, but he let me know he enjoyed listening. When the third and fourth chaplains came to visit, I detected a smile breaking out on my roommate's face. He seemed to anticipate the drama about to unfold.

The last chaplain to visit me I recognized immediately. He was one of the participants at the chaplains' conference where I had once spoken. He told me Reasons to Believe resources had often proved helpful in his ministry. He asked if any other chaplains had visited me during my stay and raised his eyebrows when I replied, "Four."

"That never happens here," he said. "Most patients get one visit, if that, unless they're here for more than a week." He asked what we had talked about during those visits, and a broad smile lit his face. "You can count on me to follow up with each of them." With that, I went home to recover, aware that my path had again been guided—and that *always* still means *always*, even if I'm sporting a hospital gown.

Channeling Darkness

A different kind of heart trauma came from navigating our children's teen years. My younger son, David, developed remarkable drumming skill by age 16, and word got out to other local musicians. (Unfortunately, the chapel director at his Christian high school never invited him to play for chapel.) The speed and power with which he could play sent heavy metal guitarists and vocalists his way. He enjoyed practicing and performing with them because of the nonstop intensity of the workout it gave him. "Better than going to a gym," he said.

Kathy and I felt a pang of concern when David started practicing and booking gigs with a band called Channeling Darkness. It's no secret that heavy metal and death metal musicians often drift toward deep spiritual darkness, including the occult. We prayed earnestly about how to handle this situation without alienating either David or his new friends.

An idea came from my research into cosmic darkness: dark matter and dark energy. One evening as practice wound down, I asked the guys if they'd like to hear about the dark stuff that comprises more than 99 percent of the universe. They responded with an enthusiastic "yes."

For nearly an hour they listened intently as I described the different kinds of cosmic darkness: ordinary dark matter, exotic dark matter, and the more recently discovered dark energy. I also let them know how the exact features, quantities, and locations of dark matter and energy provide powerful evidence of exquisite fine-tuning. Without it, we humans wouldn't be here, and we wouldn't even know what kind of universe we live in, I said.

"What do you mean?" one of them asked.

I then described how our Milky Way Galaxy is extraordinarily dark compared to other spiral galaxies and that our solar system resides in the darkest location where life could conceivably exist. Otherwise, we'd be unable to detect the radiation left over from the cosmic creation event. My comments about how cosmic darkness allows us to see the light of creation led to a discussion of how facing up to the spiritual darkness within us allows us to see our need for the Light of the World, Jesus Christ.

I had no idea how my willingness to share with them about how to channel darkness in ways they had not considered before impacted them. I soon found out. A few months later, at a concert bravely attended by Fazale and Amy Rana along with Kathy and me, the band gave a shout-out to me and performed a new song they'd written, based on that night's conversation. We still pray that each of these young men will continue to seek light throughout their life.

Never Give Up

You already know from my personal story in chapters 4 and 5 that I was the first in my family to come to Christ. But, I haven't described how my parents reacted to my commitment. I wanted desperately for them to share in my faith and joy, but they did not. More than once I overheard my mother's comment to a friend, in person or on the phone, "Hughie's got religion, but I expect he'll get over it."

Every time I tried to talk about my faith with my parents, my mother (the nurse) would immediately interrupt. She had three favorite lines:

> # Spiritual darkness within us allows us to see our need for the Light of the World, Jesus Christ.

1. Christianity can't be true because the Trinity is a mathematical impossibility.
2. If there's a God, he doesn't know what he's doing because he lets good people die and bad people live.
3. If your God is loving and just, he'd do something about all the evil and suffering in the world.

My readiness to answer these objections to Christianity did not matter because she would never allow me to give them. Her main tactics to shut me (and Kathy) down: walk away, change the subject, or loudly declare that no answer I might give could possibly suffice.

When I made the decision to leave Caltech and take a position at my church in Sierra Madre, my parents expressed deep disappointment. Why would I throw away all my wonderful education and ability, they wondered. But, they said they wanted me to be happy, and if being in ministry was my choice, they'd accept it. A year or so later, when they learned I had fallen for "a Yankee" (referring to Kathy), they realized with some sadness I'd likely be staying in California. Once they met Kathy, though, they seemed genuinely pleased.

On their occasional visits, they saw the love that surrounded us and heard stories assuring them that my science training had not gone to waste and our ministry seemed to benefit others. So, when we launched Reasons to Believe, they expressed their support. Besides, my new opportunities to travel might bring me more often to see them in Vancouver.

Whenever a ministry opportunity brought me anywhere near my parents' home, I'd stay with them in my old room. On one such visit, my mother announced that three of her dear friends from nursing school in Montreal had moved nearby, two to the Vancouver area and one to Vancouver Island, and wanted to meet me. The first time they came over, I could tell that they wanted to talk about my ministry and my beliefs, but my mother's persistent interruptions shut down any possibility to do so.

One of the three came to the house again during my next stay. This time, she had a plan. As soon as my mother left the room to put on the teapot and prepare some refreshments, she leaned toward me and whispered, "Let's talk, fast."

During those few minutes, this friend fired off her big questions: Was I certain the Bible is true; did Jesus's death and resurrection really cover all of her sins; how could she be sure of eternal life with God.

I spoke as quickly as I could in answer to all three. Then my mother returned with tea and treats, and the conversation returned to health and family and such. But, as soon as my mother excused herself for a trip to the bathroom, the two of us bowed, and I led her in a prayer of commitment to Jesus Christ as her Lord and Savior. She took a few more minutes to seek clarification that the Holy Spirit now lived within her and to ask about water baptism. When my mother rejoined us, her friend said, "Time to go home, Dot," and left.

The very next day, Mum's other two nurse friends showed up for tea. To my astonishment and delight, the previous day's scenario repeated itself quite precisely, with the identical outcome. And my mother had no idea.

As I headed to bed that evening, I realized God might have a bigger plan for my parents than I had asked for. He had already worked through my mother's hospitality to open a door for her friends. *What else does he hold in store?* I wondered. He showed me some of "what else" a little more than a year later.

That's when a Christian ministry to public high schools in the greater Vancouver area invited me to speak at their annual dinner honoring two hundred student body leaders. It would be held downtown in one of the city's finest hotels. My father offered to accompany me, and the hosts graciously allowed. My topic: scientific evidence for God.

After my talk and the formal Q&A session, I engaged students informally, responding to their more personal questions. During that time, I noticed my father near the back of the room also in deep discussion with a handful of students. Later, after wrapping up my conversations, I moved toward him and heard my father explaining to these students the benefits of giving their life to Christ, especially at this stage in their life.

On our way home, I asked my dad if, or when, he had committed his life to Christ. "I haven't," he said. "I'm not ready yet, but those students were, and I've heard you speak enough times I knew what to tell 'em."

Apparently, God is so eager to reach open hearts, he'll even use someone who's "not ready, yet."

The Christmas Gift

After Christmas the following year, my father phoned to thank Kathy and me for our Christmas gift, which had included some videos. He told me one of them had really impacted my mother, the one on the problem of evil and suffering. Dad said, "All the way through it your mom kept asking, 'Why didn't Hugh tell us this years ago?' and I wanted to say, 'Because you wouldn't let him!' but I bit my tongue."

He told me the video seemed a good way to communicate with my mum. She couldn't interrupt, and to leave the room meant extricating herself from her comfy new recliner. So, I sent a few more. According to my dad, she seemed willing to accept that Christianity offers a rational perspective on why a loving God would allow, for a time, evil and suffering to enter his creation. From another video she found an explanation for how God could be three and one simultaneously.

> **God is so eager to reach open hearts, he'll even use someone who's "not ready, yet."**

Breakthroughs were happening, but soon they would be tested. Mum's favorite brother, my uncle Herb, had gone into a hospital on Vancouver Island, where he lived, for surgery to repair an old shoulder injury. The surgery went fine, we were told, but three days later came heartrending news. Herb was gone. A staph infection had swept through his body and taken his life.

Over the years, Herb and his wife, my aunt Audrey, had become serious followers of Jesus Christ. Audrey, knowing the closeness of my relationship with Herb, asked me to speak at Herb's memorial service, officiated by their pastor. The comforting assurance of his presence with the Lord mitigated Audrey's shock and sorrow over Herb's sudden death, and I know my mother noticed.

"When I die," she said, as we drove away from the church, "I want you to give that same message."

"But Mum," I replied, "that message only fits someone who belongs to Jesus Christ."

She answered, "I'm getting there."

Within months, my mother's decades-long battle with cancer and multiple rounds of chemotherapy were taking their toll, leaving her weak and virtually incapacitated. True to her spunky character, she continued to joke and laugh with fellow patients at her care facility. When Kathy and our sons and I came to visit, she made every effort to cheer us, telling some of her goofy jokes to Joel and David. Then she turned serious for a moment.

"All my life I've neglected God and prayer," she said. "Now my body is so decrepit, I can't do much of anything else. I'm going to make up for lost time. I'm going to devote the rest of my life to praying for you and others."

She passed away at age eighty-two. During her last days, my nephew overheard a conversation between her and one of her old friends. I'll let my nephew tell the story in his own words.

At Last

My grandparents were hard people. They were hard in the sense that they firmly believed they did not require assistance from anyone. They could handle life themselves. For them, life was simply a matter of working harder and grinding through any of the obstacles that came their way. Cancer for decades? No problem. Fortitude will carry you through. Losing your pension at the end of your career due to physical injury caused by that career? Bring it on.

As a Christian I can tell you that this personality type is one of the most difficult to present the gospel to. Why? Who needs Jesus when pride and self-sufficiency falsely tell you that you don't?

At the end of my grandparents' lives (I lived with them until they passed away) I had the opportunity to witness God's handiwork. The first time was a few months before my grandmother died. She had a friend over, and they were enjoying a casual conversation. Something regarding the topic of God came up, and I braced myself for my grandmother's typical I-don't-need-religion sort of response. To my astonishment, she replied to her friend, "Jesus Christ is my personal Savior!" Thus began a spiritual conversation I never expected to hear. I wasn't around to hear how it ended, but her friend seemed quite receptive.

My grandfather lived for a few more years after my grandmother died. He, too, acknowledged and accepted Jesus Christ as his personal Savior during those last few years of his life.

The amazing thing about God is that he is always working. One of my favorite things about being a Christian is to be continually reminded of this reality. With my grandparents, God reminded me not once, but twice.

Chapter 12

Readiness Together

My initial comments on 1 Peter (in chapter 1) emphasized that the word "you" connected with "hope" is a plural. I want to amplify the point that this letter was written not to individuals, primarily, but to churches—faith communities, primarily "house churches" back then. So, the exhortation, "always be ready to give a defense" when someone asks us for "a reason for the hope" (NKJV) that we have, applies to faith communities today as well, in all their varied shapes and sizes. Think of the boost we could make toward the *billions* God showed John in his transcendent Revelation if we, as a church, were to take up this challenge!

I smile inside as I recall the first time I successfully corralled one of my Caltech colleagues to attend a church service with me. Not having gone to church before, he had no idea what to expect. And that explains why, in the middle of Pastor Anderson's sermon, my friend shot up his hand—and kept it up. Of course, this action startled everyone near us, and I heard a few muffled chuckles. However, I'll always be grateful for my pastor's response. When it dawned on him that this raised hand signaled a question, he paused mid-message and answered it. Whew! Later my friend confessed the one thing about church he found stranger than the singing was the one-way communication. Not his idea of a learning environment.

Another story that moves me deeply comes from not one person but many people I know who grew up in the church, made a commitment to Christ, were baptized, and participated in church activities for a while, but now see no reason to continue attending, other than an occasional wedding or funeral. They've heard the Bible stories and certain favorite verses and yet little to nothing about their reasons for hope, their faith's deep roots, and the church's exciting role in God's grand plan for the ages.

Movement in a healthy direction begins with a question. How ready are we, in our gatherings for worship and teaching and ministry, to invite and address questions about the basis for our hope? Rather than quote more statistics or dwell on more tales of woe about the condition of church in the West, let's put our energy and creativity to good use. Let's start *being* the church we want to see—ready, willing, and able to let our hope shine so brightly that people want to ask why we have such hope in Jesus Christ.

Welcome Doubts

Kathy and I once heard a heartrending story from our son Joel. He met a young man who made painfully caustic remarks about Christians and church. When probed for an explanation, the young man described his one experience of going to a church youth group meeting. Raised outside the church with only hearsay about what Christians believe, he came with questions—hard questions—probably asked in a less than polite way. The leader shut him down and suggested they talk privately after the group meeting. During that interaction, the flustered youth pastor essentially denounced the nonbeliever for his lack of faith and told him never to come back. Our son felt mortified to hear this but, having witnessed harsh treatment in his own youth group experience, had little to say, other than to commiserate.

Not all pastors and church leaders see doubts as a sign of spiritual weakness or rebellion. Many view questions and doubts as signs of spiritual health, even as signs of spiritual growth to help their members develop readiness. In his unique and timely book, *Room for Doubt: How Uncertainty Can Deepen Your Faith*,[1] my friend Pastor Ben Young reminds all of us to encourage, rather than discourage, expression of doubts—our own or others'. To ignore them or hide them does damage. When we bring them into the open, we invite the Lord to lead us toward answers and, at the same time, enhance our readiness to help others with their doubts and faith challenges.

I view doubts the same way I do anomalies in science research. Because we lack complete understanding of anything in nature, even the best scientific models include a few pieces of data that don't seem to fit. These anomalies present us with opportunities to dig deeper, to discover what we may have missed and come up with more complete and accurate explanations. Along the path toward an accurate understanding, the anomalies progressively shrink.

Likewise, because we lack complete understanding of the Bible and all that it reveals, doubts are inevitable. As with anomalies, doubts present us with opportunities to dig deeper, to check for some truth we may have overlooked. Doubts become powerful tools for testing and either affirming or revising our understanding of Scripture and of God's character and purposes. Through the expression of doubts and the subsequent hard work of seeking resolution, non-believers can overcome their faith barriers and believers can grow more secure in their faith, thus better equipped to reach others for Jesus Christ.

Welcome Questions and Dialogue

Timothy Keller, well-known author and church leader, took a creative approach to pastoring in the heart of New York City. He added an open mic public Q&A session to his Sunday morning agenda, and it proved wonderfully successful in two ways. First, his willingness to publicly take questions rolled out a welcome mat to doubters and skeptics. Second, it helped members of his congregation hear from people's own mouths what issues they struggle with and how to respond wisely. Keller's experiment succeeded in another way, too. It became a model for other pastors and churches. Where it has been employed, it has drawn new people in.

Doubts become powerful tools for testing and either affirming or revising our understanding of Scripture.

One Sunday at a church near one of the University of California campuses, the pastor announced a room and a time for asking questions and discussing the ideas presented during the regular worship service. Set for a half-hour after the benediction, the timing gave people the opportunity to greet friends, pick up their children, and grab a snack, while I (the speaker that day) conversed at the door with those who could not stay. The results of this experiment exceeded all expectations. The overflow crowd included many people new to the church. Our lively exchange continued for more than an hour, and a new weekly series of classes grew out of that gathering.

The offer to field live questions may seem risky, but it shows our confidence that Christianity can withstand all challenges and any degree of testing. If a question stumps us, we can admit it and ask for an opportunity to do further study before attempting to answer. In this way people see that no matter how deeply any of us delves into a subject, we always have more to learn. Sometimes we may want to assemble a panel of participants in replying to questions. This option broadens the range of thoughtful answers. Whatever the situation, we must keep in mind the importance of choosing respondents who consistently demonstrate gentleness and respect, even when the questions veer into divisive, controversial areas, such as science.

Welcome Science

What can seem more divisive and controversial in Christian circles than science? This perception explains why science avoidance permeates our faith community. The result of this avoidance is a pervasive assumption that science poses a threat to our Christian faith. Sadly, it also leads to the pervasiveness of "default atheism" within the science community.

My Reasons to Believe colleagues and I attend many science conferences where we meet few, if any, other followers of Jesus Christ. The scientists at these meetings always express surprise to discover that we are Bible-believing Christians. From their perspective, research science and atheism are synonymous. We've actually heard some say, "I'm a scientist, so I guess I'm an atheist."

At a recent conference on the origin of life, Fazale Rana and I talked with at least five scholars who said they'd never considered the possibility that a person could be a quality research scientist and a Bible-believing Christian. They initially wondered about us. However, once they learned where we earned our degrees and did our postdoctoral research, that we keep current on the scientific literature, and that we engage secular peers on both scientific topics and science-faith issues, they became willing to talk with us about the possible integration of science and Christianity. Some ended up asking for our business cards and wrote down our web address.

Our interaction with these scientists reminded me of my conversation with a paleontologist after a debate we did on a university campus. "I've always called myself an atheist," he said, "but in all honesty, I get so much enjoyment from my research I never really give any time to thinking about God or life after death or the ultimate purpose of the universe and my life." He acknowledged that for many scientists, like himself, research can be more addicting and distracting than the most captivating video games.

These encounters underscore the falsehood of the widely held perception that most scientists have decided against belief in God, in Christianity, specifically, and that the remainder are committed skeptics. Rather, they simply haven't taken the time to give the subject of God, Christianity, the Bible, or the purpose of life much serious thought or investigation. Given the opportunity to talk with someone who has thoughtfully and critically investigated these topics and is prepared to discuss them with gentleness, respect, and compassion may open a distracted researcher's mind to considering God's existence and, more importantly, God's purposes for creating the universe, life, and humans in particular.

Science avoidance on the part of the church helps convince nontheists that they *own* science. Firsthand reporting from the Reason Rally in Washington, DC, supports my point. This event, sponsored by major atheistic and secular organizations, drew large crowds of "freethinkers" to the National Mall. Reasons to Believe chapter members in the DC area also attended, holding placards or wearing T-shirts that invited conversation:

- What persuaded you that reason excludes God?
- What would it take to persuade you that God exists?

The consistent answer to both questions: "science." Conversations with these nontheists (and a few antitheists) reveal their belief that science has ruled out any need for God's existence. As I described in chapter 11, I heard the same conclusion at the 2008 International Skeptics Society conference.

These conclusions by nontheists and antitheists made me all the more thankful for those pastors, teachers, and ministry leaders who do express enthusiasm for legitimate scientific research, who welcome scientists and engineers into their fellowship, who take time to interact with them about their work, and who enlist them in ministry. Let's dispel the false notion that nearly all scientists are atheists or agnostics who are strongly opposed to Christianity.

Let's also stop being so quiet about science in the church. Christianity is not the enemy of science, and we know this fact from any review of the history of science. Nor is science the enemy of the Christian faith. Science remains our strong ally, an ally that the Bible exhorts us to embrace.[2]

> **Science avoidance on the part of the church helps convince nontheists that they *own* science.**

Welcome the Arts

In addition to incubating the scientific revolution, the church also once nurtured the revival of theater. In fact, church served as the stage, and Scripture, the script for the rise of dramatic arts in the late Medieval period. Church choirs emerged from the same fertile soil, along with painting, sculpture, and other art forms. Biblical scenes and themes dominated Medieval and early Renaissance art. Given the power of art in its various forms to move us, emotionally and spiritually, why not include creative arts in our outreach endeavors today?

Science remains our strong ally, an ally that the Bible exhorts us to embrace.

I've seen art used effectively to deliver an apologetics punch, simultaneously countering objections to the Christian faith and communicating core elements of the gospel. I'm especially grateful for the work of Max McLean, whose exquisitely crafted theatrical productions have spiritually impacted hard-to-reach audiences in major cities from New York to Los Angeles and in London, as well. On a smaller scale, I look to innovative churches like the one I visited in Perth, Australia, or to my home church in Sierra Madre, California, to experiment with drama and comedy, too, on Sunday mornings and at other times, too.

In Perth, Australia, where the divide between Christians and non-Christians seems especially hostile, comedy serves as a powerful tool to break down spiritual barriers. Humor cuts through pride and adds an element of surprise. I'll never forget being warned by the pastor to be ready for interruptions during my message. Studying an outline of my talk in advance, he and his team saw exactly where to break in—at points where my words would most likely meet with resistance. At precisely planned moments, actors would pop up, literally, from trapdoors in the stage, sometimes in crazy costumes, to dialogue with me in a comedic and yet pointed way. These interludes gave people in the audience time and context to assimilate the meaning of my message and consider how it might apply to their lives. This strategy worked so effectively that video recordings of some of the church messages began to show up on one of the Australian Broadcasting Corporation's national television network channels.

During recent months, the Sunday morning message at my home church sometimes included a captivating dramatic monologue. The speaker would

choose an obscure character in a biblical narrative, then role-play that character, switching back and forth from character to narrator simply by turning his
body around in an exaggerated way. By this means he brought to light insights
that none of us had ever noticed, igniting our thoughts and sparking conversation around spiritual points of the passage. Many newcomers have returned for
more since his first message in this engaging mode.

I look back to the time when two young artists combined their talents to
create an ambitious theatrical production in a church building across the street
from our main sanctuary. John Eldredge, a professionally trained actor and
enthusiastic new believer, wanted to put on a play that would speak to his nonbelieving friends and get them thinking, but without being preachy. He met
a professional scriptwriter, Frank James, in our congregation, who shared his
vision and stepped up to help, and the two of them pitched their idea to the
pastoral team.

Permission was granted, and their first production, *A Christian Carol* (obviously a Dickens spin-off) brought people to our church who might never
have come to a Sunday service, and they didn't just applaud and go home. John,
Frank, and the actors and actresses served refreshments and interacted with the
audience (a sellout crowd) between the three acts and also afterward, asking
them questions about what they had just witnessed and experienced. People
stayed long after the proverbial curtain drop, and the Holy Spirit opened hearts.

In all, more than forty people in our church who had never been involved
in outreach participated. Some helped with sets, others with costumes, some
with refreshments, others with promotion and ticket sales. One of the biggest
benefits of this venture came from the message it sent to the entire church family: evangelism takes many different forms, and every Christian can use their
unique talents and gifts to communicate God's truth, life, and love with people
who do not yet have a relationship with Jesus Christ. If the evangelism form
that fits you doesn't already exist, do what these two did—invent it! With all
the talented artists in the church today, I see potential for creative new ways to
answer apologetics questions and break through resistance to faith.

Seeker Sensitivity

Like any other living entity, the church grows in stages and through phases. What
"church" looks like depends to some extent on time and place and demographics. Today, the recognizable pattern for "doing church" in the West (or in places
where Western influence holds sway) involves two main components: the large
Sunday gathering for worship and small groups that meet during the week.

The worship service we're most accustomed to, with anywhere from a few dozen to a few thousand people, includes an extended time of congregational singing, a prayer or two (plus one for the offering), announcements, perhaps a video clip or special music, and then a ±30-minute sermon, followed weekly or monthly by communion (the bread and the cup).

This familiar church pattern is so common, we tend to forget that not everyone in the sanctuary (or whatever the meeting space may be called) knows what's going on and why. People who come from different faith traditions or no faith at all may feel very much like "outsiders," confused and eager to bolt. Only the spiritually desperate or intensely curious or dutiful spouses hang in. Recognition of this fact has moved many churches toward becoming "seeker sensitive."

These days, pastors and guest speakers more often show thoughtfulness toward the individuals who may not know how to find a particular passage in the Bible or understand references to Calvary, much less basic doctrines and creeds. I hear less condemnation and more identification with the self-absorption that keeps *all* of us from a deeper relationship with our Creator and Savior. However, I also hear more "Christianity lite" (watered-down and distorted versions of Christianity) and, in some cases, I see a heavier emphasis on glitz and glamour and entertainment (overly produced, spectacularly flashy worship sets).

I'm all for making church more inviting and exciting to nonbelievers, especially those who assume it must be dull and depressing. What in the world—or the universe, for that matter—could be more thrilling and downright gripping than a real-life encounter with the living God? If stories, illustrations, lights, music, dancing, and humor help facilitate that encounter, rather than distract or detract from it, then praise God. But we can learn a lot by tuning into what people are thinking about and talking about on their way out the door, and we'd do well to listen.

Teaching that is spiritually challenging and intellectually stimulating to the most mature and biblically literate people in the sanctuary carries a far more enduring and valuable impact than anything I can think of. When seekers see that even longtime believers find their faith fueled or stretched by the message, their own faith may be ignited. They see a reason to come again and a hope that what Christ offers really does exceed the value of any other treasure the world holds dear. They recognize that walking with God means to become more fully alive every day, no matter the circumstances.

A Discovery or Foundations of Christianity class series, by whatever name we want to give it, can enable seekers to "catch up" on what they've missed, the basics they need to know about the foundations of our faith, what the Bible covers and why we can trust it, the ups and downs of church history, what distinguishes the Christian worldview from all others, and some of the differences and divisions we're still working to settle while keeping a vibrant witness to the world. My dream would be to see such classes offered regularly, and open to all ages, not just adults, at every church. What a resource this series could be in helping newcomers get grounded in the basics of Christianity—and in preparing believers to give reasons for our hope to those who ask!

Small Group Focus

Aware that personal relationships—knowing and being known—play a vital role in spiritual vitality and growth, churches have worked hard to establish and multiply small groups. "Small" typically means 6–12 people, meeting weekly for a time of fellowship and refreshments that includes Bible study and prayer, in a home, office, or designated room at the church, or elsewhere. A number of churches provide a sermon-related or themed curriculum for these groups to follow, while others allow groups to decide what they'll focus on.

The relational depth these groups foster make church feel more like family, and this family atmosphere tells the world that Christ's followers genuinely love one another. God has worked through these groups to help some people who thought they were Christians because they attended church to learn the real meaning of discipleship. What I think these groups may be missing, however, comes from the thrill of teamwork in outreach. They may be overlooking their exciting potential to lead nonbelievers, including those with no church background, to Christ. Nothing does more to create deep bonds than this type of interaction.

With a vision for this potential and a desire to help groups step into this vision, Reasons to Believe, among other ministries, has produced videos specifically for use in a small group setting. Christians and non-Christians meet together for eight weeks or so, to watch a video segment and then discuss the content and questions it presents. Exciting reports of these videos' impact have come back to us, and I encourage small group leaders to consider using them.[3] They equip and evangelize simultaneously, and that's their unique strength.

My greatest yearning is to mobilize more believers to get personally involved as teams, such as small groups, in advancing Christ's kingdom. I've already seen some of what can happen when believers put their creativity and skills and interests to use in outreach. Some of the ideas (which sprang not from my imagination, but from the innovative ideas of my colleagues, as well as of Reasons to Believe chapter members) appear in my closing chapter.

Mid-Sized Group Possibilities

Let's step into the shoes of the nonbeliever who feels totally alone, out of place, and invisible in a typical church service or uncomfortably exposed, as if a spotlight shines directly on them, in a small group. With some additional entry points for both believers and nonbelievers into the faith community, something in between these two alternatives, we can draw more people in—especially people with little to no church background.

Mid-sized groups, including Sunday classes and midweek Bible studies, help address the challenges of anonymity and lack of opportunity for engagement in the large group and exposure in the small groups. Groups ranging from 25 and 75 participants allow non-Christians to listen and observe inconspicuously. If structured appropriately, such groups invite non-Christians to enter into discussion and dialogue, when they feel ready, without drawing more attention to themselves than they want. Some of these individuals need several opportunities to blend into the woodwork and inconspicuously watch how Christians engage one another. They need multiple assurances that their questions or comments will be handled graciously. They need to see what happens when Christians express their questions and spiritual struggles.

Depending on their experiences and expectations, nonbelievers may test the group leader—and the group—by raising arguments popularized by some well-known atheists before venturing to ask their own questions. When this happens, the well-prepared leader and readied group may be poised for a significant breakthrough opportunity. A calm and positive response from the outset sets the tone. If the leader and the group show care for the "challenger" and eagerness to discuss the difficult issue presented, their response builds trust, and God can work mightily in a wounded heart or confused mind. The more class members who jump into prayer (rather than panic) at such moments, the better.

Mid-sized groups have existed in some churches for years, and the great advantage they offer, in addition to serving as onramps for nonbelievers, lies in their adaptability—what I view as their potential for experimentation. The Paradoxes Sunday School Class (paradoxes.org) in Sierra Madre, California, represents a four-decade-long experiment,[4] and it continues to yield results (the main reason to keep an experiment going). The class fits no description I've found in a textbook on outreach, and yet it works. And I'm convinced it can be replicated, or at least approximated in an effective way.

This particular group includes all ages, from 9 (or younger) to 99 (or older) and has always been intergenerational. About half of the attendees also regularly attend church, and the rest come from widely diverse backgrounds, spiritually and otherwise. A core group anchors the class, but others come and go from week to week, month to month, and year to year.

A team shares the leadership and teaching. We tend to choose a theme and then work our way through everything the Bible has to say on that subject. However, on any given Sunday the leader is encouraged to exercise the option of giving precedence to engaging questions raised by people in the class or from the live-streamed audience, especially if it comes from one of the children, newcomers, agnostics, or atheists. Their courage to ask often frees other class members to jump in. Engagement between members of different generations encourages everyone, including me, to think about and process questions that may never have occurred to us at the stage of life we're now in.

On a quarterly basis, this group hosts what amounts to a skeptics forum. These outreach events begin with an introduction of the rules and a brief commentary on some recent scientific discovery with spiritual significance, but as soon as a line forms at the microphone, questions become the focus. Our ground rules are simple. Rule #1: No "softball" or "fake" questions raised to target someone in the room. Rule #2: One question at a time, not a string of questions. (However, return trips to the microphone are allowed.) People too apprehensive to come to the microphone can text their questions to the moderator or write them on the 3" x 5" cards provided. Rule #3 (the easiest rule to follow): Help yourself to refreshments (provided by class members) at any time.

The two-hour time limit always seems to run out before the questions (and refreshments) do. And conversations sometimes continue until the custodial crew arrives. We consistently see God at work in these gatherings, and the class finds them helpful in their readiness training. Recently a young Muslim heard about the forum and joined in. Without hesitation, the group welcomed him, even though he returned to the microphone at least six times. As the session wrapped up, he shared that for months he had searched for Christians who'd hear and answer his faith questions, but to no avail. With tears he thanked me and the group for meeting his deep desire to learn what Christians believe about the triune God, about how to please him, and about life after death.

More Experiments

In my travels around the country to speak, I enjoy seeing some of the different experiments churches are running to see what draws in "inquirers," especially those with little or no church background. In one city, I experienced a café-type arrangement—people seated around tall and short tables, enjoying light snacks and beverages, taking notes on their laptops and tablets, and texting questions to the pastor. Another provided awnings and gazebos on the lawns outside the church building where little ones could play and parents and others could watch the service on large video screens.

Several churches are making good use of theater space, school auditoriums, or even lounges to draw people in. Others have returned to the "house church" approach of early believers. These neutral environments convey the message that church does not mean a building. It means people committed to growing closer to God and learning how to love others, including their enemies, as Jesus loves us.

Children and Youth Readiness

My views on what children's ministry would best prepare young ones to grow up as effective ambassadors for Christ may be considered iconoclastic, and yet I wonder what will become of future generations of believers if we don't change things up a bit in this area of church ministry. There is nothing wrong with snacks and crafts and Bible stories, but have we considered how much attention we give to helping kids discover who God is and how to build a relationship with him? As my friend Patty says, lesson after lesson "teaching them to be good" can actually be a hindrance to their spiritual growth. If doing and saying the right things pleases God and makes them "good," how can they ever identify with their need for a Savior, their need of "amazing grace that saved a wretch like me"?

Given that young brains work best with concrete objects rather than abstract concepts, study of the natural realm (aka science) seems an obvious way to draw

> **Church does not mean a building. It means people committed to growing closer to God and learning how to love others.**

kids toward the God who reveals himself and speaks to us through the book of nature. Here, as with the skeptics forum idea, we have an opportunity to let curiosity lead the way. What do kids' interests tell us about where to start introducing them to who God is and how he loves and provides for them? What do their fears and fantasies tell us about what we need to address with them?

If nothing else, I hope my questions will spur some youthful, talented communicators and budding scientists to collaborate in creating fresh curricula for Sunday school, vacation Bible school, and student ministries. The "Cosmic Clubhouse" Vacation Bible School program featured by one or more local churches that partnered with us this past summer seems a step in this exciting direction.

Of all the reasons I could give, or have given, for churches to become more welcoming to men and women of science, technology, engineering, and mathematics (STEM), the demand for their knowledge and experience, especially among children, preteens, teens, and twentysomethings, ranks highest. While the interests of these young people certainly do cover a broad spectrum (sports, music, movies, fashion, video games, etc.), a Barna Group survey finds that 52 percent of teens who regularly attend church youth group meetings look forward to STEM careers.[5] Meanwhile, the same Barna Group survey reports that these teens' youth group leaders and teachers devote a mere 1 percent of their contact time to STEM topics or science-faith issues.[6] This gap underscores the misconception that science and related fields belong to the secular world, not the sacred. To some extent the future of the church rests in our readiness to change this message.

God has designed every component of his creation to display some aspect of his care, and each holds a unique fascination for the human observer. Thus, we can easily engage both young and older minds with some newly discovered feature or fact of nature. If we can make a connection between that discovery and one of God's attributes or a component of God's plan to redeem humanity, we will have provided a stronger motivation for people to seriously investigate the book of Scripture.

As I shared in an earlier chapter, the book of nature brought me to the book of Scripture, which led me, in turn, to submit my life to the Redeemer, Jesus Christ. I am not alone. I have met many others who came to Christ in a similar way. Some Christians are amazed to hear how frequently I get to share my faith with strangers. To a large degree, God uses the book of nature and the links he reveals between nature's record and key components of his redemptive plan to open up these opportunities.

Attending to the Arrival Gate

I cannot blame pastors for wanting to avoid conflict and controversy and to keep peace in their congregations. Most people recoil from conflict. However, many pastors, out of fear that members of their congregations may choose to depart, go so far as to refrain from addressing topics that may, potentially, stir up heated differences of interpretation and opinion.

Unfortunately, avoiding conflict is like avoiding the dentist or doctor in hopes of ignoring possible cavities or health problems. Conflicts, like dental and medical issues, come up eventually, and the longer they are ignored, the worse they are guaranteed to be.

Peacemaking, as contrasted with peacekeeping, faces conflicts head-on and seeks resolution. Peacemaking takes hard work, laboring to transform clashing parties into full allies. Peacemaking seeks creative alternatives to either-or choices. It assumes the best motive, truth-seeking.

In 2 Corinthians 5:19–20 we read that God has "committed to us the message of reconciliation. We are therefore Christ's ambassadors, as though God were making his appeal through us." Clearly, this passage refers to the role of Christians in spreading the message of salvation, and yet I see wider implications, as well.

Christians can help people receive the message of reconciliation to God by modeling reconciliation among themselves. John 13:35 says, "By this everyone will know that you are my disciples if you love one another." How well do we show love when we disagree? Nonbelievers look on and wonder if they can trust Christians to deal gently and respectfully with their questions and doubts if we don't treat each other that way. Part of "keeping a clear conscience" means committing ourselves to reconciliation. As we talk openly, honestly, and humbly on issues that divide us and work together lovingly in the pursuit of resolution and reconciliation, nonbelievers will see that we can help them be reconciled to God, as well as to others with whom they may disagree.

Because pastors take their shepherding role seriously, they may be tempted to show more concern for the few who might leave over a conflict or controversy than for the many more who will likely come if it's addressed and resolved in a respectful and compassionate manner, with an unswerving commitment to go where the evidence leads. They read Matthew 18:12–14 as their mandate to keep any sheep from wandering away. However, not all who look like sheep really are. A few goats and wolves may camouflage themselves convincingly for a while, but their lack of submission to Jesus Christ shows through when they begin to stir up dissension and division rather than participate in seeking resolution. I believe God wants pastors to keep an eye on the departure gate, especially if damaged relationships can be repaired, but also to give equal or greater priority to the arrival gate, bringing in lambs and sheep who have yet to discover their true identity in Christ.

Special Occasions

Even people who never darken the church door on a Sunday will attend a wedding. What an opportunity this occasion gives us not just to tell but also to *show* the gospel! Revelation 21 calls the community of believers "the bride of the Lamb." The groom represents Christ by committing himself to love his bride, caring and providing and protecting sacrificially and enduringly for her. The bride exemplifies the church, including the individual believer, responding to Christ's love by committing herself unreservedly to him.

Part of "keeping a clear conscience" means committing ourselves to reconciliation.

Whenever I officiate a wedding, I invite the guests to follow the bride's example in saying "yes" to our groom, Jesus. But the teaching opportunity doesn't end there. The wedding offers a chance to look back at the very first earthly marriage, the one that joined Adam and Eve. I like to describe how God allowed Adam to recognize his lack of a partner, a "not good" situation (God's words, Genesis 2:18). Then, because God is our *ezer* (the Hebrew word for his power to defeat any foe), he provided the just-right counterpart to Adam, an ally in fulfilling God's purpose for humanity.

Note how soon (Genesis 3) the man and woman meet their enemy, the evil one. Even though they succumb to his wiles and suffer the consequences, God remains their ally—as he remains ours. By bringing up this topic at weddings, I'm hoping to give a clear spiritual focus not only to the newlywed couple but also to the Christians present. I'm hoping they will talk more about God's plan for marriage—an alliance between bridegroom, bride, and the Holy Spirit to thwart God's enemy by advancing God's kingdom—as they converse during the reception and after.

As with weddings, everyone attends a memorial service or funeral once in a while. As Ecclesiastes 7:2 says, "a house of mourning" brings a beneficial reminder that "death is the destiny of everyone." Many people take the easy but dangerous path of putting off any thoughts about preparation for the inevitable.

If asked to officiate a funeral or graveside service, I try to answer at least one nagging question in some depth: what is it like to die? I explain that the death experience for a Christian differs from that of a nonbeliever. For a Christian, death holds no fear of impending judgment for sin. For Christians, rewards and a welcoming embrace await. God sometimes blesses believers for a few hours during the last few days of their life on Earth with an experience of surpassing peace, comfort, and anticipation. An abundance of eyewitness reporting suggests that in the moment of death, Jesus calls his own by name and personally escorts them across the threshold from nature's realm into his presence, an indescribably greater realm. There they meet all the believers who've preceded them, their eternal family, and the celebration goes on.

Scripture supports this observation. One example appears in the book of Acts. In the story of Stephen's execution by stoning, we read that Stephen saw heaven open and saw Jesus standing at the Father's right hand. This sight gave him the peace, security, and compassion to fall on his knees while he was being stoned and shout out, "Lord, do not hold this sin against them" (Acts 7:55–60).

For the non-Christian, however, the anticipation of judgment for sin brings the opposite of peace. To some it brings terror—and one final opportunity to call out for their Rescuer—while to others, it brings blasphemous defiance. According to Ezekiel 18:24, God actually blesses those who've rejected his grace by ignoring their "good works," all done to glorify self rather than God. He chooses not to count their so-called good deeds against them. (See also Isaiah 64:6–7).

Memorials and funerals highlight the fact that we're all given a choice in the kind of death we'll experience and where we will spend eternity. Whether death comes suddenly and unexpectedly, or slowly after long years, it comes. So, *today* is the time to prepare.

Baby dedications and believers' baptisms and other special occasions with spiritual significance also bring people through the church doors and into contact with believers. Each of these events highlights the need for readiness. Each provides an object lesson depicting the source of our hope and potentially prompts questions about it. As we bathe these occasions in prayer, God will use them to draw people in.

Prioritize Prayer

As we Christians pray together in groups, I can't help but notice our tendency to focus more on physical needs than on spiritual concerns. I mention this point not to condemn. After all, physical needs have a certain tangibility and urgency to them. Spiritual needs seem harder to identify and articulate. Imagine what can happen if all believers were to make a conscious, concerted effort to give spiritual illness and injury more attention and higher priority in our prayers, individual and corporate. Personally, I have yet to meet anyone or any group who prays too much.

Every believer I know is calling on God for the salvation of family members and friends, even for people whose names we don't know. And yet, how often do we ask God for his guidance in how to pray for them, what he plans to do, and whom he may want to use in bringing them to faith? God encourages us to be specific so we can see him at work and rejoice with even the smallest step toward trusting in him. He may show us through prayer how he will intervene to bring someone to faith in Jesus Christ. He wants us to understand and commit to our role and to support others in their role as he brings a person to himself. Through our prayers God may reveal the steps, timing, and circumstances through which he is working.

In the case of my own parents, for example, my prayers for their salvation stretched out over a span of more than thirty years. Initially, I simply asked God to save them. But then I asked Kathy and others to join me, and we began asking the Lord to help us pray more specifically and effectively for them. I longed for some clues as to how, when, and in what way God would bring them to faith in him. Recognizing that God typically uses human messengers and human relationships, my prayer partners and I began to pray they would meet other Christians, believers in their age range and with similar interests and likable personalities. They did. When I heard my parents express dismay over friends' marriages falling apart, God showed us to ask for a Christian couple whose marriage they would respect and admire to come into their life. They came. When I sensed God asking me to take initiative or to back off, I did my best to obey. At times, I invited them to events. At other times, Kathy and I sent them books or videos. When we sensed God asking us to show more patience, we pressed him to help us understand the importance of the long wait. He eventually showed us.

Through this experience of praying for my parents, and others, too, and celebrating step by step how he intervened, God affirmed for me that his plans and goals consistently surpass our own. We want a friend or relative to become his follower. God wants that friend or relative to come in a time and a way that brings more people to faith in him. On rare occasions, he may even use a person's resistance or rebellion in the process of bringing others to repent and submit their lives to their Creator-Redeemer. An obvious scriptural example comes from the story of Egypt's pharaoh at the time of Moses. Pharaoh's rebellion and its consequences convinced many Egyptians to join the family of God (Exodus 12:38). Let's answer God's call to "rejoice always" and to "pray continually." He never ceases to hear and to fulfill his purposes. What a privilege to play a part!

Chapter 13

Readiness and Demeanor

Perhaps you've noticed that in many translations of 1 Peter 3:15–16, the word "but" or "yet" appears immediately after the exhortation to be ready for questions. Have you ever wondered, as I have, what makes nonbelievers so reluctant to ask questions or to visit our churches? The cautionary note Peter includes in his message deserves special attention because it shines a light on one of our weak spots.

To remain calm, gentle, and respectful in an environment where nonbelievers readily speak against, disparage, even slander Christians takes as much preparation, if not more, than readiness to give logical reasons for our faith and hope. We can easily become harsh and disrespectful, especially if questions come across as challenging or defiant. Only by the empowering Holy Spirit, the one who sets up opportunities for us to share, can we replace our natural response with a supernatural one.

Only by the empowering Holy Spirit . . . can we replace our natural response with a supernatural one.

A Personal Concern

Several of the popular evangelists and evangelism trainers I know and appreciate have adopted a certain strategy to help Christians overcome their hesitancy and lack of preparedness to give answers. They equip believers to put nonbelievers on the defensive, to trap them in their own absurdities and inconsistencies. Trainees learn to ask specific questions virtually guaranteed to expose the weaknesses and logical inconsistencies of nonbelievers' views on life and the world. The hope is that this discomfort will open a door. The person may become flustered enough to listen to a presentation of the gospel.

While a time and a place for such questions may well exist, more often than not I have seen this approach interpreted as demeaning and humiliating, rather than humbling. The believer has put the nonbeliever on the defensive. And, rather than inviting further spiritual conversation, conversation immediately shuts down—or, worse yet, turns into verbal sparring.

My suggestion may seem counterintuitive, but I think we can open more conversations by inviting non-Christians to put *us* on the defensive. By asking them questions we genuinely want to know about them, questions that may even draw an appropriate apology, we show respect and level the field beneath our feet. And we may learn what questions or topics we need to become better prepared to discuss. Here are some of the questions I've used, but I strongly encourage you to come up with your own:

1. Do you have faith questions you've never gotten good answers to?
2. What's one of the hardest things in the Bible for you to believe?
3. Where in your life do you find it most difficult to believe in God?
4. What do you think the world would be like if more people were Christians?
5. What do you find most annoying about Christians you have met?
6. What do you find most admirable about Christians you have met?
7. Assuming God does exist, what are two questions you would like to ask him?

Follow-up questions show that we're really listening. For example, if someone says, "I can't believe the Bible because it's filled with contradictions," it may help to ask which contradictions bother them the most. If the person says, "No one can prove there's a God," we might ask what kind of "proof" they'd consider helpful. Or, if they come out with the familiar refrain, "Christians are just a bunch of hypocrites," we have a great chance to learn what hypocrisy has impacted them personally.

By asking open-ended questions, we can help nonbelievers and skeptics start to feel at ease with us and trust us to be gracious. Through patient listening, we can allay the fear that we're simply trying to set them up, rather than wanting to hear from them. If we resist the urge to put them on the defensive, we may find ourselves enjoying more meaningful and fruitful conversations. And it does not mean we're wimps. We can speak uncomfortable truths, as needed for honesty's sake, but not in a triumphal way that puts the other person down.

Further Preparation

I can understand why Christians may prefer to put nonbelievers and skeptics on the defensive. This approach allows us to control the subject matter. We can steer the conversation to the reasons we feel best prepared to give. We stand a better chance of avoiding the embarrassment of being asked a question we're not prepared to answer.

I'm convinced God intends our preparation of logical reasons for our hope in Jesus Christ to continue for a lifetime. Inevitably, inviting nonbelievers and skeptics to ask their questions will bring up issues we don't yet have good answers for. These moments alert us and challenge us to study further, to keep enhancing our responses. They provide the best opportunities for improving our reasons to hope in Jesus Christ.

Whenever someone raises a question we can't answer, or answer well, we can thank them. Rather than stumble through an inadequate answer, we can admit we don't know and embrace the opportunity to research the particular subject at some depth. We can always ask for time and another chance to talk.

Friends and Strangers

I can see a second explanation, and a more favorable one, for the emergence of an assertive approach to personal outreach. It may represent a pendulum swing away from the "friendship evangelism" focus popularized in the 1980s. Church growth researchers during that era—and since—observed two dangerous trends, each a threat to the future of Christianity in the West, particularly.

The first trend emphasized a "goers vs. senders" approach in spreading the good news of salvation in Jesus Christ. Christians began to look upon going and sending as if they represented *either-or* categories, rather than our *both-and* calling in Christ.[1] All who support the work of evangelism, whether at home or abroad, certainly do have a share in that work and reason to rejoice in its eternally significant outcome. However, sending does not discharge our responsibility for also going, personally participating in the work of evangelism. Every believer is also called to go, but where and how? A realization of this training gap has given rise to a new emphasis on equipping believers to reach out, and I thank God for it, even if some methodologies concern me. God can use them and has used them for his good purpose.

The second trend also represented an unhealthy divide. Many committed Christians, including the most generous and enthusiastic senders, had become so wrapped up in church life and activities they had little time and energy to devote to people outside the church, and had few if any non-Christian friends. In response to this challenge, pastors and other leaders began to emphasize and encourage "friendship evangelism." Unfortunately, this term has such a nice ring to it, few bothered to define what it really means.

Again, a schism developed. Friendship and evangelism seemed to go their separate ways. Either the new "friends" came to sense a lack of genuineness to the relationship and left it, or genuine friendship developed and evangelism fell by the wayside. According to George Barna, "At any given time, a majority of believers do not have a specific person in mind for whom they are praying in the hope that the person will be saved."[2] And yet, hope remains.

Friendship evangelism holds great potential for "making disciples," the mission Jesus calls us to. Genuine friendship, rooted in God's unconditional love, cares as deeply for our friends' eternal well-being as for any other facet of their life. By persistent prayer for them and by practice in giving our *apologia* among strangers, we can optimize our readiness to speak when the Holy Spirit is stirring our friends' readiness to receive.

> **Genuine friendship, rooted in God's unconditional love, cares as deeply for our friends' eternal well-being as for any other facet of their life.**

Ambassadors for Reconciliation

As I have written in previous chapters, we Christians lack *complete* knowledge and understanding of God's revelation in the book of Scripture and the book of nature. As a result of our gaps, we often collide with fellow believers in our interpretation of either book or both books. We differ over multiple issues of faith and practice, and we differ over what we consider the best and most effective reasons for hope in Christ. When we address our differences in a healthy way, in the way of peacemakers rather than peacekeepers, we fulfill our ambassador role, as described in 2 Corinthians 5:18–20 (a parallel passage to 1 Peter 3:15–16):

> All this is from God, who reconciled us to himself through Christ and gave us the ministry of reconciliation: that God was reconciling the world to himself in Christ, not counting people's sins against them. And he has committed to us the message of reconciliation. We are therefore Christ's ambassadors, as though God were making his appeal through us. We implore you on Christ's behalf: Be reconciled to God (NIV).

Obviously this passage refers to the role of Christians in spreading the good news that through Christ's redemptive work we can be reconciled to our Creator. And yet, I'm convinced it also has wider implications. As we Christians work through our conflicts toward reconciliation with one another, we gain not only greater maturity and a deeper understanding of God's truth, but also the attention of nonbelievers who are watching us.

One way we Christians can help others receive our message about being reconciled to God is by modeling reconciliation among ourselves. John 13:35 says, "By this everyone will know that you are my disciples, if you love one another." Even though so many nonbelievers today stumble over science issues on their path to faith, no other subject seems to expose a greater lack of love among believers.

These nonbelievers wonder, *How can we trust Christians to deal with our questions and differing views when they treat each other so badly over their differences?* How, I ask, can we call people to be reconciled to God unless we show willingness to work toward reconciliation with one another in a respectful, loving manner?

I am not so naive as to think *all* the belief differences among Christians will be resolved in my lifetime. However, with sufficient confidence in the revelation God has given us in the 66 books of the Bible, and in the scientific disciplines that probe ever more deeply into the book of nature, and with sufficient humility in our efforts to integrate what God has revealed, I'm convinced we can and will make progress toward resolving our differences. If we truly behave as kingdom ambassadors in our behavior toward one another and to the world around us, we will reap a harvest of souls and gain life-changing truth from God.

Winsome Demeanor

Multiple research studies affirm that people pay more attention to how we say something than to what we say. Peter didn't need to know about these studies to recognize that the quality of our demeanor in offering reasons for our hope carries significant weight, at least as much weight as the quality of our explanations. The real challenge, as my comments about offense and defense suggest, lies in striking a balance between the extremes of boldness and reticence.

Peter's emphasis on keeping a clear conscience points the way. Guilt over secret sin, or fear of its exposure, can—and typically does—spark a reaction, rendering us defensive or judgmental or distracted. It gives the lie to our hope, which springs from God's mercy and grace. Confession, repentance, and restitution bring radiance to our hope, lighting the way to exciting opportunities.

Gentleness grows in us the way any other fruit of the Spirit grows. Think of grapes on a vine and how they grow. They soak up water provided by the grower. They stay attached to the vine, lifted up whenever it droops and pruned of extraneous shoots, again by the grower. They bask in the Sun's light and warmth, provided from above. Jesus gave us this picture (John 15:1–17) to help us understand that growth is a process in which we cooperate and he does the work.

Respect for questioners comes from steeping like a teabag in the truth of Philippians 2:5, which says, "In your relationships with one another, have the same mindset as Christ Jesus." Consider how Jesus treated the woman, the town outcast he met at Jacob's well in Samaria. Not only did he respect her by speaking kindly and gently to her, he also asked for a drink from her water jar—even more scandalous, by cultural standards. He didn't just speak with lepers and blind men; he touched them. One young pastor and evangelist shared his approach to maintaining an attitude of respect: "I look upon every person I meet as a possible brother or sister in my forever family." Kathy says she looks for "the image of God" in the face of the people she meets.

> **"I look upon every person I meet as a possible brother or sister in my forever family."**

Feedback is one thing Jesus did not need, but we can all benefit from it. My friend and colleague Mark Perez has found a way to call for feedback on the spot. When he has finished answering someone's question, he asks (in a gentle, respectful tone), "Was I responsive to your question?" In this way he opens himself to hearing whether he missed the person's point or gave only a partial or unsatisfactory answer. As I've watched him in action, I realize that by showing respect in this way, he gains respect. People listen carefully to him because he listens carefully to them.

Observing Mark and learning from him reminds me that we can all benefit from hearing feedback from those who observe us in our conversations. Some of us, myself included, may not be adept at recognizing how we come across to others. Our emotional antennae lack sensitivity. For this reason, I prefer to engage in outreach with at least one teammate, better yet with an even larger group. That's the topic I take up next, and it involves two qualities I especially prize: creativity and experimentation.

Chapter 14

The Readiness Bonus

Like all verses of Scripture, Matthew 28:19 (the familiar Great Commission verse) resides within a larger context. We forget sometimes that New Testament chapter and verse markers came into use simply for readers' convenience, most likely between the thirteenth and sixteenth centuries. When a statement carries the weightiness of Jesus's final command to his followers, it may tend to overshadow its surroundings. I noticed this effect recently in rereading the final portion of Matthew 28.

There we read that the eleven remaining disciples made their way to a certain mountain in the Galilee region, where Jesus had arranged to meet them. The passage continues, "When they saw him, they worshiped him; but some doubted." The doubters worshiped, despite their doubts. At this moment, we see how the risen Christ, who knows every thought and intent of these eleven hearts (1 Chronicles 28:9), responds to worshipful doubters. Not with a rebuke. Not with a repeat of his earlier offer (to Thomas) of tangible evidence. Instead, he proclaimed his divine authority over heaven and earth and said, "Go and make disciples of all nations . . ."

This response sends a message I seldom hear. It comes through most clearly in Paul's letter to Philemon, verse 6: "I pray that the sharing of your faith may become effective for the full knowledge of every good thing that is in us for the sake of Christ" (ESV). Paul points to a connection between communicating our faith and deepening our confident grasp of how good and wonderful God's gift to us in Christ really is. In other words, sharing our faith expands our faith.

Countless believers will testify that even the process of preparing to give good reasons for our hope in Jesus Christ deepens our knowledge of the riches we have access to in him. If we lack a solid case for our hope, it will grow as we prepare. If we've forgotten some of what God once taught us about his trustworthiness, this getting-ready-to-give-answers process will refresh and solidify that memory. If we struggle with feelings of hopelessness, we have an opportunity to explore what experience(s) or false beliefs interfere with our ability to hang on securely to an unshakable hope.

Sharing our faith expands our faith.

The practice of sharing reasons for our hope in Christ with people who don't yet know him reveals what kinds of reasons people whose backgrounds differ from our own need to see or hear before they're willing to trust in Christ. Awareness of what hinders their faith fuels our motivation for ongoing study and sharpens our communications skills. It also reveals how God works through us even though we communicate imperfectly.

Personally, I have gained more knowledge and understanding of Scripture and theology through the experience of interacting with nonbelievers about my reasons for hope in Christ than through any other spiritual discipline.

Benefit to Bystanders

In chapter 4, I mentioned brief instances during my growing up years when I heard a Christian's words as he spoke about his faith with other people. In those instances, the person speaking had no idea I'd heard what he said or that his words stuck and eventually impacted my spirit. This realization encourages me deeply. It tells that when I'm expressing my reasons in conversation with one person, the Holy Spirit may be speaking hope to someone nearby, someone I have no awareness of at the time.

Sometimes this invisible spillover effect becomes obvious. As I mentioned in some of my air travel stories, eavesdroppers sometimes spoke up and asked questions of their own, based on overheard conversations with other passengers. At times I'll notice someone has stopped paying attention to their electronic device and started leaning toward me. Most of the time, though, I have no idea who's paying attention to what I'm saying. The Holy Spirit will use whatever he chooses to bring light to someone's heart, and the timing belongs to him.

More Benefits from Doubts

"Doubting Thomas" holds a special place in my heart. Like many engineers, researchers, and other thinkers, Thomas needed evidence to believe the utterly unbelievable—"unbelievable" from a strictly natural perspective, that is. However, the moment he received the clear evidence of supernatural reality, he jumped into faith with both feet, "My Lord and my God!" His disbelief did not come from a rebellious heart. So, we're reminded not to make unwarranted assumptions about the hearts of those who ask for evidence.

The Matthew 28 passage assures us that seeing and hearing and touching the supernatural may still leave us with doubts. We've heard the saying, "If it sounds too good to be true, it probably is." The two men who traveled with Jesus all the way to their home in Emmaus certainly must have felt that way. Jesus walked with them and taught them, from Scripture, about himself—even while they failed to recognize him. He did call them out for their unbelief of the prophets' words. But he showed them great patience and opened their minds.

Jude 22 says, "Be merciful to those who doubt." I thank God for the pastors and church leaders who mercifully acknowledge questions and doubts as signs of spiritual health, even as signs of spiritual growth. As I mentioned in chapter 12, tackling doubts is an effective means for gaining more truth and deepening our faith.

Pretending we don't have doubts leads to danger. Behind this pretense lies a deep-seated fear that good answers may not exist. If by "good answers" we mean "absolute proof," we need to think again. Absolute proof is an impossible standard. None of us has, or will have, absolute proof of anything because we do not and cannot know everything. However, God has given us abundant *practical* proof. He has provided *sufficient* evidence for the certainty of our hope. So, if we pursue answers and resolve our doubts, with God's help, our awareness of practical proof will grow.

Some Christians feel embarrassed to admit doubts because they've been told that if they just had enough faith, they'd harbor no doubts. They worry that people might find out about their doubts and, consequently, think less of them as

> **Pretending we don't have doubts leads to danger. Behind this pretense lies a deep-seated fear that good answers may not exist.**

Jesus's followers. If we meet someone who struggles in this way, let's be ready to remind them that since God knows our doubts already, we have nothing to lose and everything to gain by admitting them and asking for help.

Readiness may involve finding out what attribute of God a nonbeliever finds most difficult to accept. Is it God's power? God's love? God's goodness? When I pay attention to people's doubts, I discover questions in my own mind that I've not yet fully resolved. This new awareness leads me to dive more deeply into reflection and study, to persist in wrestling with God for answers, and thereby to grow. Call me weird, but I get excited when I hear a doubt expressed that I've not heard before. As I've said before, a new doubt is a new opportunity to learn something about God I have yet to comprehend.

Deepening Answers

Continuing the practice of sharing our faith in Christ will, at times, expose the weakness or superficiality of an answer we've thought was good. The moment a person reacts to it and shows us its weakness can be painful, for sure. However, *if* we humbly listen to people's disappointments with our answers, we'll gain more opportunities to grow.

Imagine what can happen if each one of us continues developing more thorough and helpful answers to people's doubts about God for the rest of our days. God is infinite. We can never, in this life, fathom the depths of his being. Call me selfish, but I find preparing and offering reasons for hope in Christ the most spiritually rewarding of all adventures.

Benefits of Scripture Memory

With the Bible and all kinds of search tools now easily accessible on the internet, I can understand why people may lack motivation to memorize Scripture. Bible memorization may be a nearly lost discipline, but it still has its place. The longest chapter in the Bible, Psalm 119, makes a lengthy list of benefits that come from storing up the Word of God in our hearts, all of them beneficial to our readiness to give reasons.

According to this Psalm, memorizing Scripture, that is, storing up God's Word in our hearts (v. 11) will keep us on the path of purity (v. 9); help us live according to God's ways (v. 10); guard us from sin (v. 11); help us discover wonderful truths (v. 18); strengthen us to withstand scorn, contempt, and slander (vv. 22–23); broaden our understanding of God's truth (vv. 32, 104); turn our eyes away from worthless things (v. 37); produce reverence (v. 38); preserve our life (v. 40); bring us hope and comfort (vv. 49–50); enable us to see that the earth is filled with God's love (v. 64); reveal the value of affliction (v. 71); affirm God's enduring faithfulness (v. 90); light our way along life's path (v. 105); provide peace and security (v. 165), among many other wonderful blessings.

Bible memorization resembles language acquisition. The adage "use it or lose it" applies. Disuse has caused my fluency in French to evaporate. I now struggle even to read French, whereas I once could converse in it. Scripture passages I rarely use, I tend to forget.

On the other hand, Bible passages I use often, especially in offering people reasons to believe in Christ, I do not forget. Frequent use actually takes much of the work out of memorization. I find that if I use a Bible passage multiple times in answering people's questions about faith, that passage gets locked in my mind. Other Christians tell me they experience this same effect. Given the number and magnitude of benefits that accrue from storing up the truths of Scripture, the advantages of using Scripture when we offer reasons for our hope in Jesus Christ cannot be overstated.

Nothing but Benefits

For years, psychologists have produced lists and hierarchies of things people fear most. No doubt you've heard, time and again, that "social phobias," such as public speaking, top the list. Why? The pain this fear touches upon runs deep— so deep it drives some people to behave in desperate ways.

Jesus put his finger on this pain and transformed it into something else, the final "blessed" in his Sermon on the Mount, the Beatitudes:

> Blessed are you when people insult you, persecute you and falsely say all kinds of evil against you because of me. Rejoice and be glad, because great is your reward in heaven, for in the same way they persecuted the prophets who were before you (Matthew 5:11–12).

Nothing pierces the soul quite like ridicule or being *maligned* (yes, it's "malignant"). Speaking up to give reasons feels risky, and more so with time. Christians in other parts of the world face this risk to a much greater degree, of course. But insults and accusations can cut to the heart, nonetheless, especially attacks aimed not at what we've said or done but, rather, at who we are at the core. That's why bullying, for example, so deeply wounds those whose sense of self has yet to mature in a healthy way. That's why the evil one makes deadly use of these weapons.

However, the core of a believer, the new "self" God creates in us, is exactly where Christ lives, by the Holy Spirit. And he assures us that the cutting words, when and if we do encounter them, aim directly at him, not us. So, by his power and presence, by "the whole armor of God," the fiery darts fall harmlessly to the ground. Because of the cross and the resurrection, they have no power to harm. Instead, joy rises up in us, not *from* us but *in* us. It rises from the One who sees beyond what we can even imagine—the reward that awaits us in his presence.

Even taking ridicule for our ready reasons to hope in Christ brings us closer to him. Jesus calls us "blessed" in that moment. He uses this weapon of the enemy to bring a unique experience of joy and gladness. When my Caltech officemate, Ian Lockhart, ridiculed my beliefs, it stung, but I also sensed God might be working on him. Then, when he told the astronomers in the break-room that he could no longer ridicule my belief in the God of Bible because he had dedicated his life to Jesus Christ, a tidal wave of joy and gladness swept over me. That joy and gladness lasted not just days or weeks but months and years, especially as the change in Ian's life opened many more opportunities to share my reasons for my hope in Jesus Christ. Speaking up is worth the risk.

> **Even taking ridicule for our ready reasons to hope in Christ brings us closer to him.**

This entire book represents an attempt to encourage all believers to share in the benefits of developing readiness, always, to give reasons for the hope that we have in Christ. Its deeper purpose is to demonstrate God's readiness to intervene on behalf of his people for his kingdom's advance. He's the one who arranges appointments, and empowers us to keep them, the moment we're ready. He wants to bless us with these encounters.

However, he does not toss any of us into the proverbial "deep end" of the faith-sharing pool without allowing us to wade in, float around a little, blow some bubbles, and take a few basic strokes with the assistance of others. Remember, he won't let you sink, and he won't let you drown anyone, either. So, I close this book with some suggestions for getting started, if you haven't already.

Chapter 15

Ready for Action

"How beautiful on the mountains are the feet of those who bring good news." Isaiah wrote these words, and Paul repeated them in Romans 10:15, to underscore the privilege of giving reasons for our hope in Jesus Christ. Bringing good news is a beautiful thing not only to the people who receive it, but also to the people who do the bringing.

The beauty of giving reasons becomes evident and grows once we start. So the sooner we start, the better. If anything from my experience—or my friends' and colleagues' experiences along the way—can help break inertia and propel you forward, please pick it up, shape it according to your personality, and use it to God's glory. No perfect mold or model exists; so no need to worry about breaking it. Every work of hope-building art God creates is unique.

Lifelines

Whether we've engaged in a brief interaction or a long conversation, we can throw someone a lifeline by leaving them with a way to learn more. Let's leave no one dangling. Business cards work well, but so do handwritten 3" x 5" cards or whatever else may be convenient for establishing a link to further information. It may not be appropriate to give personal contact information, such as a phone number, but we can at least leave a web address or social media connection where the person we've shared with can continue to explore reasons for hope. Basic rule of thumb: don't give out another person's contact information without advance permission.

Every work of hope-building art God creates is unique.

One of my good friends and a fellow Reasons to Believe board member, Nina, carries a large handbag, not as a fashion statement but as a repository for her version of "calling cards." She packs CDs of my testimony with contact information for Reasons to Believe (RTB) on the cover. She also carries cards with information about the RTB chapters in her part of the country. Everyone Nina speaks with receives a link to additional reasons, beyond those she has shared. Some may not receive what she offers, but her Southern charm proves hard to resist. And God uses it for good.

Those of us who carry briefcases have a sizeable advantage in carrying capacity. As my stories suggest, God often allows me opportunities to give away books, booklets, or DVDs. Whether short or long, a conversation may reveal questions or interests that one of these resources addresses and, thus, the chance to offer it. Others travel light, with just pockets or small bags, but even these allow room for a few cards. A writing instrument is essential, of course.

Nothing substitutes for face-to-face discussion of faith's reasons. However, supplementing an encounter with other communication tools may well carry home the gospel to someone's heart. I cannot count all the times a person has told me God used a particular book or other resource to bring them to faith. Books and videos, including YouTube recordings, can be assimilated and savored over time. Some people need that time.

Talking about easing in, I recently met a woman who has yet to read through any of my books, yet she has given away nearly two hundred—based on her trust in my character, credentials, and track record. (Ordinarily, I'd say refrain from giving away books you haven't read and personally checked out.) She has no background in science and no aptitude for it, she says. So, when she encounters people who challenge her on the facts behind her faith, she simply admits she's unable to offer adequate answers, and then adds, "Here's a book that does."

She tells her Christian friends, "Don't wait until you can spell out all the arguments for God's existence or for Jesus Christ as Creator and Savior." A new believer can have an impact even while preparing to offer sound reasons for hope in Christ. When the Holy Spirit prompts us to give a resource to relatives, friends, or coworkers, our ongoing relationship gives us opportunities for personal follow-up. We can let them know that we, too, are still checking out the resource and would like to get together over coffee/tea or lunch sometime soon to discuss our thoughts.

Ramping Up

My unusual circumstances in coming to faith in Christ meant "going it alone" (in partnership with the Holy Spirit, of course) when I first began to answer questions and offer reasons. For the vast majority of believers, however, God has already provided teammates and coaches. Teams of two or ten or more can develop effective outreach opportunities, creative plans, and projects the rest of us might never think of. Here, I offer just a few examples of the many developed by RTB chapter members, as well as by other friends and colleagues.

Family field trips

The availability of an expert who can see and describe apologetics connections in their sphere of study opens all kinds of outreach possibilities. A group of Christians near Fresno, California, for example, organized an outing around the topic of plate tectonics. It included a picnic near a tectonic fault line and discussion with a geologist, who spoke about evidence for God's exquisite design of Earth's crust.

Believers who live near one of the great museums, zoos, or fossil beds in our country may want to arrange a visit focused on dinosaurs or primates or some other creature(s) of special interest. I mention these two for a reason. Dinosaurs fascinate kids and bring up all kinds of questions about Earth's changing environment and animal populations through time. Primates lead easily to discussion of what differentiates us humans from them, despite striking and entertaining similarities. Such visits provide great opportunities to talk openly about the topic of evolution, about the many distinct ways the word is used, how controversies have arisen, and why it remains such a contentious issue. To lead this kind of discussion requires both a calm disposition and careful preparation. RTB offers videos that can help.

Observatories, planetariums, and aquariums also make good field trip sites. Psalm 19 sets the theme for discussion either before, during, or after an observatory visit. No one has to stretch to connect objects in space to discussion of God's handiwork. For night owls, staying up late to see the Perseid meteor shower in August or the Geminid meteor shower in December can also lead to some significant conversations. Sea creatures hold a fascination of their own. They, too, leave us in awe of the Creator's artistry.

Star parties

Anyone who owns a telescope knows that just setting one up can draw a small crowd. One or two telescopes can easily substitute for an observatory visit, with

no cost or other complications. Near big cities like Los Angeles, stargazing usually means a short drive into the mountains or desert, but many locations offer
dark enough skies for good viewing. A telescope helped Kathy and me meet
our neighbors and their children. We've found that even if the Moon and the
planets are the only things we can observe due to light conditions, there's no
problem. It opens conversation about the uniqueness of Earth's Moon, and
how the just-right characteristics of our neighboring planets make our life on
Earth possible.

Some members of the RTB Austin, TX, Chapter regularly set up a number
of telescopes on a popular-with-pedestrians bridge over the Colorado River
near mid-city. Each time they do, God gives them plentiful opportunities to
speak with curious passersby. Some have never spoken at length or in-depth
with a Christian. Many show surprise to meet Christians interested in astronomy, or any other science for that matter. Cards are always available for those
who'd like to talk further or check out a chapter meeting.

Adventure trips

Whether backpacking, camping, hiking, river rafting, kayaking, sailing, or
some other activity, adventures create opportunities for bonding and more in-
depth conversation than most everyday schedules typically allow. Kathy and
I have seen people come to Christ or take steps closer to him each time we've
participated in an outing of this kind with other believers alongside us. In one
case, seeds planted during a river adventure took more than ten years to sprout
and bear fruit, but God nurtured and watered them all the way. We just learned
that a fellow rafter was baptized this past year.

Our friend Mark Clark recently went on what appeared at first glance a
"failed" hunting trip (no quail for dinner) with a small group of men, some
younger, some older. During their weekend together, one of the guys who had
grown bitter and withdrawn over the death of a loved one opened up for the
first time, shared his pain, and a mighty work of healing began in his heart. Each
man participated in the process, one way or another, and each felt God's touch.
Several in the group described this trip as an encounter with God. Sometimes
people need time away from their routine to attend to their secret struggles.

Special interest clubs

If two or more Christians share a keen interest in anything, it can become an
opportunity for relationships that lead to spiritual influence. The possibilities
cover a wide spectrum from reading, to writing, to classic cars, to cooking, to

Sudoku, to board games, to something far beyond this list. Even if an interest group agrees to meet just a few times per year or some other limited time frame, much good can come of this interaction.

Service clubs, whether church-based or community-based, seem especially conducive to interaction and conversation in which we Christians can share our worldview and values and the reasons for our hope. When Kathy served on a local school site council with other parents and school administrators, her conversations with the one other Christian serving on that council stirred the curiosity of others. God gave these two some exciting opportunities to share their reasons for hope.

School support groups

Retirees and others who have flexible schedules and love kids have banded together to provide after-school tutoring at a nearby public elementary school. In addition to helping with homework, they give their time and attention to children who hunger to be known, and if the children ask spiritual questions, the helpers have the freedom to answer.

A few years ago, a group like this in the Long Beach area looked for a way to minister to the teachers and staff at a beleaguered public school near their church. They began by organizing a teacher appreciation event, with the principal's consent. Then they discovered other ways to help, providing supplies not covered in the school's tight budget and providing backpacks for underprivileged kids. These efforts to give, with no expectation of return, and no pressure to attend their church, made a huge impact on many nonbelievers in that school community and led to many spiritually productive conversations.

Truth-seekers club

Try asking a group of teenagers raised in church, "How do you know that Christianity is true?" One courageous colleague of mine, Krista Bontrager, ventured to ask a question like this of her daughters' friends. She ached to realize some of these kids might end up as statistics in the growing "no-longer-interested-in-Christianity" category.

Krista's rare combination of credentials allowed her to launch a group by herself, but if a few passionate individuals were to pool their spiritual resources and relational skills, I'm confident they would make an eternal difference in some young lives, especially if committed to learning right alongside the students. Many of the resources Krista has developed through the years can be found online at reasons.org in the education category.

Another young friend and pastor, Ryan Bohm, has put together a Bible literacy course for the students in his church and any interested friends. He occasionally teams up with other adults to address topics the students are asking about, and I've personally observed the work God is doing among these young people. Ryan welcomes anyone interested in launching a similar study to contact him at Sierra Vista Community Church in Upland, California.

> **Whatever comes of our efforts comes *from* the Lord—and *for* his glory, alone.**

Stepping Out

Rather than add more examples to this list, I want to encourage every reader to create examples of their own, to write living stories of how God works to prepare people *to receive* as well as to give reasons for hope in him. We know that whatever comes of our efforts comes *from* the Lord—and *for* his glory, alone. My prayer for you is the same one Paul prayed for the believers in Rome centuries ago, when the body of Christ withstood every effort to crush it:

May the God of hope fill you with great joy and peace as you trust in him, so that you may overflow with hope by the power of the Holy Spirit (Romans 15:13).

To share your story of how *Always Be Ready* or RTB helped prepare you for a divinely orchestrated encounter, visit **reasons.org/shareyourstory.**

Ready for Hospitality

Because the Holy Spirit indwells every person who is *in Christ*, every believer is "gifted" to serve as an ambassador for God's kingdom. In other words, we're all gifted to serve as purveyors of the good news that Jesus Christ has redeemed us from sin and death to eternal life, beginning here and now. So, the opportunity and capacity for evangelism belongs to every Christian, even though each Christian expresses this gift in a unique way.

The gift of hospitality provides a helpful ministry comparison. While some Christians seem to be especially adept at offering what we familiarly think of as hospitality—welcoming, feeding, and sheltering guests—all Christians have a part to play in showing hospitality to others. God calls each of us to be hospitable, whatever our personality and circumstances. Thus, Christian hospitality takes many forms.

In his letter to the Roman church, Paul urges believers in their hostile environment to "practice hospitality" (Romans 12:13) in such a way as to "bless and do not curse," "rejoice with those who rejoice; mourn with those who mourn. Live in harmony," and "be willing to associate with people of low position" (Romans 12:14–16). Peter, likewise, exhorts believers scattered across Asia Minor and beyond, "Offer hospitality to one another without grumbling" (1 Peter 4:9).

One reason Christ calls every one of his followers to the ministry of evangelism *and* hospitality is to help each of us grow spiritually, developing more and more the mind and character of Christ (Romans 12:1–2). He knows that even with the empowering Holy Spirit and his many gifts available to us, evangelism and hospitality demand sacrifice and humility. Such demands are good. Growth in Christ is all about sacrifice and humility. As we mature in sacrifice and humility we become more effective, productive, and joyful in both evangelism and hospitality.

I see an obvious synergy between the two. Evangelism and hospitality go hand in hand. Just as evangelism is more than outlining "the sinner's prayer" (as important as that may be in appropriate circumstances), hospitality is more than offering someone food and drink and a place to rest.

Christian hospitality involves serving others' needs at all levels of their being—physically, intellectually, emotionally, and spiritually—typically in that order, but not always. It entails developing a close partnership with the Holy Spirit that enables us to discern what specific needs of the individual should be addressed first.

Christian evangelism involves close partnership with the Holy Spirit in discerning where a person stands in relationship to our Creator and then assisting that individual to take a step closer to a life-giving, personal relationship with him. It begins with questions designed to draw out the individual's most significant barriers to faith or to a deeper, more fulfilling relationship with Christ. It progresses to an understanding of the individual's perception of and encounters with these barriers. It leads to discerning where to start in addressing and resolving barriers, checking frequently to ensure that the resolution reaches the needed depth and breadth. Discerning, addressing, and resolving an individual's barriers may take several encounters over a considerable period of time. By keeping in step with the Spirit we can recognize when and how to clarify the meaning of *repentance* and the truth of total forgiveness for sin—past, present and future. Our great hope is that we can guide someone into an eternally secure, loving, and fulfilling personal relationship with Jesus Christ, and yet the process doesn't stop there. It means continuing to assist and encourage that individual in Christian growth to maturity.

> **Christian hospitality involves serving others' needs at all levels of their being— physically, intellectually, emotionally, and spiritually.**

Hospitality enhances the effectiveness of this entire process. Hospitality means being available to listen and to create an environment where an individual can easily and safely open up. Food, drink, a relaxed environment, a sensitivity to personal needs, a demonstration that you genuinely care, and, most importantly, the investment of your time and attention—that's what hospitality is all about. God can and often does use such hospitality, especially when it's ongoing, to facilitate a nonbeliever's spiritual transformation and enduring spiritual vitality.

Bibliography

Books

Geisler, Norman. *When Skeptics Ask: A Handbook on Christian Evidence*. Rev. ed. Grand Rapids, MI: Baker Books, 2013.

Guillen, Michael. *Amazing Truths: How Science and the Bible Agree*. Grand Rapids, MI: Zondervan, 2016.

_____. *Can a Smart Person Believe in God?* Nashville: Thomas Nelson, 2006.

Habermas, Gary. *The Risen Jesus & Future Hope*. Lanham, MD: Rowman & Littlefield, 2003.

Keller, Timothy. *The Reason for God: Belief in an Age of Skepticism*. New York: Viking, 2008.

Lennox, John C. *God's Undertaker: Has Science Buried God?* Oxford, UK: Lion Hudson, 2009.

McDowell, Josh, and Sean McDowell. *Evidence That Demands a Verdict: Life-Changing Truth for a Skeptical World*. Nashville: Thomas Nelson, 2017.

_____. *77 FAQs about God and the Bible: Your Toughest Questions Answered*. Eugene, OR: Harvest House, 2012.

Murray, Abdu. *Grand Central Question: Answering the Critical Concerns of Major Worldviews*. Downers Grove, IL: IVP Books, 2014.

Qureshi, Nabeel. *Seeking Allah, Finding Jesus: A Devout Muslim Encounters Christianity*, exp. ed. Grand Rapids, MI: Zondervan, 2016.

Rana, Fazale. *Creating Life in the Lab: How New Discoveries in Synthetic Biology Make a Case for the Creator*. Grand Rapids, MI: Baker Books, 2011.

Rana, Fazale, and Hugh Ross. *Origins of Life: Biblical and Evolutionary Models Face Off*. 2nd ed. Covina, CA: RTB Press, 2014.

Ross, Hugh. *Beyond the Cosmos: The Transdimensionality of God*. 3rd ed. Covina, CA: RTB Press, 2017.

_____. *The Creator and the Cosmos: How the Latest Scientific Discoveries Reveal God*. 4th ed. Covina, CA: RTB Press, 2018.

_____. *Hidden Treasures in the Book of Job: How the Oldest Book in the Bible Answers Today's Scientific Questions*. Grand Rapids, MI: Baker Books, 2014.

_____. *Improbable Planet: How Earth Became Humanity's Home*. Grand Rapids, MI: Baker Books, 2016.

_____. *A Matter of Days: Resolving a Creation Controversy*. 2nd ed. Covina, CA: RTB Press, 2015.

_____. *More Than a Theory: Revealing a Testable Model for Creation*. Grand Rapids, MI: Baker Books, 2012.

_____. *Navigating Genesis: A Scientist's Journey through Genesis 1–11*. Covina, CA: RTB Press, 2014.

_____. *Why the Universe Is the Way It Is*. Grand Rapids, MI: Baker Books, 2008.

_____, Kenneth R. Samples, and Mark Clark. *Lights in the Sky and Little Green Men: A Rational Christian Look at UFOs and Extraterrestrials*. Colorado Springs: NavPress, 2002.

Samples, Kenneth R. *7 Truths That Changed the World: Discovering Christianity's Most Dangerous Ideas.* Grand Rapids, MI: Baker Books, 2012.

_____. *God among Sages: Why Jesus Is Not Just Another Religious Leader.* Grand Rapids:, MI: Baker Books, 2017.

_____. *Without a Doubt: Answering the 20 Toughest Faith Questions.* Grand Rapids, MI: Baker Books, 2004.

_____. *A World of Difference: Putting Christian Truth-Claims to the Worldview Test.* Grand Rapids, MI: Baker Books, 2007.

Willard, Dallas. *The Allure of Gentleness: Defending the Faith in the Manner of Jesus.* San Francisco: HarperOne, 2016.

Young, Ben. *Room for Doubt: How Uncertainty Can Deepen Your Faith.* Colorado Springs: David C. Cook, 2017.

Zweerink, Jeff. *Is There Life Out There?* Covina, CA: RTB Press, 2017.

Booklets

Rana, Fazale, and Hugh Ross. *What Darwin Didn't Know.* Covina, CA: Reasons to Believe, 2009.

Ross, Hugh. *Genesis One: A Scientific Perspective.* 4th ed. Covina, CA: Reasons to Believe, 2006.

Zweerink, Jeff. *Who's Afraid of the Multiverse?* Covina, CA: Reasons to Believe, 2008.

DVDs

Journey toward Creation. Reasons to Believe, 2006.

Evolution under the Microscope. Reasons to Believe, 2015.

Navigating Genesis Curriculum Kit. Reasons to Believe, 2014.

Notes

Chapter 1: Ready for What?

1. Kenneth S. Wuest, *First Peter in the Greek New Testament for the English Reader*, vol. 2 of *Wuest's Word Studies* (Grand Rapids, MI: Wm B. Eerdmans, 1973), 91.
2. Wuest, *Wuest's Word Studies*, 89.

Chapter 2: God's Works in Preparing Earth for Human Beings

1. Hugh Ross with John Rea, "Big Bang—The Bible Taught It First!" in Hugh Ross, *The Creator and the Cosmos*, 4th ed. (Covina, CA: RTB Press, 2018), 25–31. An abbreviated version is available at http://www.reasons.org/explore/publications/rtb-101/read/rtb-101/2000/06/30/big-bang-the-bible-taught-it-first.
2. I describe these tests and measurements in two books: *Beyond the Cosmos*, 3rd ed. (Covina, CA: RTB Press, 2017), 26–31; *The Creator and the Cosmos*, 4th ed. (Covina, CA: RTB Press, 2018): chapter 10, 114–120.
3. Stephen Hawking and Roger Penrose, "The Singularities of Gravitational Collapse and Cosmology," *Proceedings of the Royal Society A* 314 (January 27, 1970): 529–48, doi:10.1098/rspa.1970.0021; Arvind Borde, Alan H. Guth, and Alexander Vilenkin, "Inflationary Spacetimes Are Incomplete in Past Directions," *Physical Review Letters* 90 (April 18, 2003): id. 151031, doi:10.1103/PhysRevLett.90.151301.
4. Sean M. Carroll, "What If Time Really Exists?" (November 23, 2008): eprint, arXiv:0811.3772; Sean Carroll, *From Eternity to Here: The Quest for the Ultimate Theory of Time* (New York: Dutton, 2010).
5. Eric S. Perlman et al., "New Constraints on Quantum Foam Models from X-Ray and Gamma-Ray Observations of Distant Quasars," (July

28, 2016): eprint, arXiv:1697.08551, paper presented at the Fourteenth Marcel Grossman Meeting, University of Rome "La Sapienza," July 12–18, 2015, which will appear in the proceedings of the conference; Eric S. Perlman et al., "New Constraints on Quantum Gravity from X-Ray and Gamma-Ray Observations," *Astrophysical Journal* 805 (May 20, 2015): id. 10, doi:10.1088/0004-637X/805/1/10; Eric S. Perlman et al., "Using Observations of Distant Quasars to Constrain Quantum Gravity," *Astronomy & Astrophysics* 535 (November 2011): id. L9, doi:10.1051/0004-6361/201118319; Wayne A. Christiansen et al., "Limits on Spacetime Foam," *Physical Review D* 83 (April 15, 2011): id. 084003, doi:10.1103/PhysRevD.83.084003; F. Tamburini et al., "No Quantum Gravity Signature from the Farthest Quasars," *Astronomy & Astrophysics* 533 (September 2011): id. A71, doi:10.1051/0004-6361/201015808; Richard Lieu and Lloyd W. Hillman, "The Phase Coherence of Light from Extragalactic Sources: Direct Evidence against First-Order Planck-Scale Fluctuations in Time and Space," *Astrophysical Journal Letters* 585 (March 10, 2003): L77–L80, doi:10.1086/374350.

6. Aron C. Wall, "The Generalized Second Law Implies a Quantum Singularity Theorem," *Classical and Quantum Gravity* 30 (August 21, 2013): id. 165003, doi:10.1088/0264-9381/30/16/165003; Aron C. Wall, "The Generalized Second Law Implies a Quantum Singularity Theorem," (December 6, 2016): eprint, arXiv:1010.5513v5; Hugh Ross, *The Creator and the Cosmos*, 4th ed. (Covina, CA: RTB Press, 2018), 102–5, 112–13.

7. Michael R. Wilczynska et al., "A New Analysis of Fine-Structure Constant Measurements and Modelling Errors from Quasar Absorption Lines," *Monthly Notices of the Royal Astronomical Society* 454 (December 11, 2015): 3082–93, doi:10.1093/mnras/stv2148.

8. Paul Davies, *The Cosmic Blueprint: New Discoveries in Nature's Ability to Order the Universe* (New York: Simon and Schuster, 1988), 203.

9. Hugh Ross, "Your Galaxy's Diet Is Important for Your Health," *Today's New Reason to Believe* (blog), *Reasons to Believe*, September 7, 2015, reasons.org/explore/blogs/todays-new-reason-to-believe/read/tnrtb/2015/09/07/your-galaxy-s-diet-is-important-for-your-health; Igor A. Zichenko et al., "On the Influence of Minor Mergers on the Radial Abundance Gradient in Disks of Milky-Way-Like Galaxies," *Astrophysical Journal* 806 (June 23, 2015): id. 267, doi:10.1088/0004-637X/806/2/267; A. S. G. Robotham et al., "Galaxy and Mass Assembly (GAMA): In Search of Milky Way Magellanic Cloud Analogues," *Monthly Notices of the Royal*

Astronomical Society 424 (August 1, 2012): 1448–53, doi:10.1111/j.1365-2966.2012.21332.x; D. Crnojević et al., "How Unique Is the Local Group? A Comparison to the Nearby Centaurus A Group," in *Galactic Archaeology: Near-Field Cosmology and the Formation of the Milky Way*, ed. Wakō Aoki et al., *Astronomical Society of the Pacific Conference Series*, vol. 458 (San Francisco: Astronomical Society of the Pacific, 2012), 321.

10. Hugh Ross, "RTB Design Compendium (2009)," *Reasons to Believe*, November 16, 2010, reasons.org/fine-tuning.

11. Hugh Ross, "Milky Way Galaxy's Midlife Crisis," *Today's New Reason to Believe* (blog), *Reasons to Believe*, October 3, 2011, reasons.org/explore/blogs/todays-new-reason-to-believe/read/tnrtb/2011/10/03/milky-way-galaxy-s-midlife-crisis; Simon J. Mutch, Darren J. Croton, and Gregory B. Poole, "The Mid-Life Crisis of the Milky Way and M31," *Astrophysical Journal* 736 (August 1, 2011): id. 84, doi:10.1088/0004-637X/736/2/84; Lulu Liu et al., "How Common Are the Magellanic Clouds?," *Astrophysical Journal* 733 (May 20, 2011): id. 62, doi:10.1088/0004-637X/733/1/62.

12. Hugh Ross, "Our Sun Is Still the One and Only," *Today's New Reason to Believe* (blog), *Reasons to Believe*, April 17, 2017, reasons.org/explore/blogs/todays-new-reason-to-believe/read/todays-new-reason-to-believe/2017/04/17/our-sun-is-still-the-one-and-only; Hugh Ross, "Search for the Sun's Twin," *Today's New Reason to Believe* (blog), *Reasons to Believe*, March 17, 2008, reasons.org/explore/blogs/todays-new-reason-to-believe/read/tnrtb/2008/03/17/search-for-the-sun-s-twin; Hugh Ross, "Enhanced Activity in Solar-Type Stars," *Today's New Reason to Believe* (blog), *Reasons to Believe*, February 1, 2010, reasons.org/explore/publications/tnrtb/read/tnrtb/2010/02/01/enhanced-activity-in-solar-type-stars; Hugh Ross, "No Bad Flare Days for the Sun," *Today's New Reason to Believe* (blog), *Reasons to Believe*, February 6, 2014, reasons.org/explore/blogs/todays-new-reason-to-believe/read/tnrtb/2014/02/06/no-bad-flare-days-for-the-sun; Hugh Ross, "Middle Age Is Good, Especially for Our Sun," *Today's New Reason to Believe* (blog), *Reasons to Believe*, October 24, 2016, reasons.org/explore/blogs/todays-new-reason-to-believe/read/todays-new-reason-to-believe/2016/10/24/middle-age-is-good-especially-for-our-sun.

13. Hugh Ross, *Improbable Planet: How Earth Became Humanity's Home* (Grand Rapids, MI: Baker, 2016), 166–68.

14. Linda T. Elkins-Tanton and Sara Seager, "Ranges of Atmospheric Mass and Composition of Super-Earth Exoplanets," *Astrophysical Journal* 685

(October 1, 2008): 1237–46, doi:10.1086/591433; Hugh Ross, "Planet Formation: Problems with Water, Carbon, and Air," *Today's New Reason to Believe* (blog), *Reasons to Believe*, January 11, 2009, reasons.org/explore/blogs/todays-new-reason-to-believe/read/tnrtb/2009/01/11/planet-formation-problems-with-water-carbon-and-air; Hugh Ross, "Too Much Water Is Bad for Life!" *Today's New Reason to Believe* (blog), *Reasons to Believe*, November 7, 2016, reasons.org/explore/blogs/todays-new-reason-to-believe/read/todays-new-reason-to-believe/2016/11/08/too-much-water-is-bad-for-life!.

15. Ross, *Improbable Planet*, 78–93; Hugh Ross, "'Electric Wind' Becomes 9th Habitable Zone," *Today's New Reason to Believe* (blog), *Reasons to Believe*, July 4, 2016, reasons.org/explore/blogs/todays-new-reason-to-believe/read/todays-new-reason-to-believe/2016/07/04/electric-wind-becomes-9th-habitable-zone.

16. Yoko Ohtomo et al., "Evidence for Biogenic Graphite in Early Archaean Isua Metasedimentary Rocks," *Nature Geoscience* 7 (January 2014): 25–28, doi:10.1038/ngeo2025; Fazale Rana and Hugh Ross, *Origins of Life: Biblical and Evolutionary Models Face Off* (Covina, CA: RTB Press, 2014): 70–75.

17. L. E. Snyder et al., "A Rigorous Attempt to Verify Interstellar Glycine," *Astrophysical Journal* 619 (February 1, 2005): 914–30, doi:10.1086/426677; Yi-Jehng Kuan et al., "A Search for Interstellar Pyrimidine," *Monthly Notices of the Royal Astronomical Society* 345 (October 21, 2003): 650–56, doi:10.1046/j.1365-8711.2003.06975.x; Hugh Ross, "Natural Sugar Synthesis?" *Today's New Reason to Believe* (blog), *Reasons to Believe*, August 6, 2007, reasons.org/explore/publica,tions/tnrtb/read/tnrtb/2007/08/06/natural-sugar-synthesis.

18. Hugh Ross, *Improbable Planet*, 94–107; Kevin D. McKeegan, Anatoliy B. Kudryavtsev, and J. William Schopf, "Raman and Ion Microscopic Imagery of Graphitic Inclusions in Apatite from Older than 3830 Ma Akilia Supracrustal Rocks, West Greenland," *Geology* 35 (July 1, 2007): 591–94, doi:10.1130/G23465A.1; Allen P. Nutman and Clark R. L. Friend, "Raman and Ion Microscopic Imagery of Graphitic Inclusions in Apatite from Older than 3830 Ma Akilia Supracrustal Rocks, West Greenland: Comment," *Geology* 35 (January 1, 2007): e169, doi:10.1130/G24384C.1; Kevin D. McKeegan, Anatoliy B. Kudryavtsev, and J. William Schopf, "Raman and Ion Microscopic Imagery of Graphitic Inclusions in Apatite from Older than 3830 Ma Akilia Supracrustal Rocks, West Greenland: Reply,"

Geology 35 (January 1, 2007): e170, doi:10.1130/G24987Y.1.

19. Niles Eldredge, *The Triumph of Evolution and the Failure of Creationism* (New York: W. H. Freeman, 2000): 35–36.

20. Richard N. Boyd et al., "Sites that Can Produce Left-Handed Amino Acids in the Supernova Neutrino Amino Acid Processing Model," *Astrophysical Journal* 856 (March 21, 2018): id. 26, doi:10.3847/1538-4357/aaad5f; Hugh Ross, "Natural Source of Life's Homochiral Molecules?" *Today's New Reason to Believe* (blog), *Reasons to Believe*, April 30, 2018, reasons.org/explore/blogs/todays-new-reason-to-believe/read/todays-new-reason-to-believe/2018/04/30/natural-source-of-life-s-homochiral-molecules.

21. Hugh Ross, "Homochirality: A Big Challenge for the Naturalistic Origin of Life," *Today's New Reason to Believe* (blog), *Reasons to Believe*, October 2, 2017, reasons.org/explore/blogs/todays-new-reason-to-believe/read/todays-new-reason-to-believe/2017/10/02/homochirality-a-big-challenge-for-the-naturalistic-origin-of-life; F. C. Frank, "On Spontaneous Asymmetric Synthesis," *Biochimica et Biophysica Acta* 11 (March 12, 1953): 459–63, doi:10.1016/0006-3002(53)90082-1; Jose J. Flores, William A. Bonner, and Gail A. Massey, "Asymmetric Photolysis of (RS)-Leucine with Circularly Polarized Ultraviolet Light," *Journal of the American Chemical Society* 99 (May 1977): 3622–25, doi:10.1021/ja00453a018.

22. Rana and Ross, 70–78, 164; Minik T. Rosing and Robert Frei, "U-Rich Archaean Sea-Floor Sediments from Greenland—Indications of >3700 Ma Oxygenic Photosynthesis," *Earth and Planetary Science Letters* 217 (January 15, 2004): 237–44, doi:10.1016/S0012-821X(03)00609-5; Minik T. Rosing et al., "The Rise of Continents—An Essay on the Geologic Consequences of Photosynthesis," *Palaeogeography, Palaeoclimatology, Palaeoecology* 232 (March 22, 2006): 99–113, doi:10.1016/j.palaeo.2006.01.007.

23. Derek C. Penn, Keith J. Holyoak, and Daniel J. Povinelli, "Darwin's Mistake: Explaining the Discontinuity between Human and Nonhuman Minds," *Behavioral and Brain Sciences* 31 (April 2008): 109–30, discussion 130–78, doi:10.1017/S0140525X08003543.

Chapter 3: Ready for What?

1. John F. MacArthur, *Charismatic Chaos* (Grand Rapids: Zondervan, 1992); Walter J. Chantry, *Signs of the Apostles: Observations on Pentecostalism Old and New* (Edinburgh: The Banner of Truth Trust, 1978); Benjamin B. Warfield, "The Cessation of the Charismata," in *Counterfeit Miracles*

(New York: Charles Scribner's Sons, 1918), 1–32. These authors argue that the completion of the New Testament canon, the infallible and sufficient authority of the Bible, and the perfection of Scripture to guide Christians and the Church did away with the need for the confirmatory miracles recorded in the book of Acts.

2. Kenneth S. Wuest, *First Peter in the Greek New Testament for the English Reader*, vol. 2 of *Wuest's Word Studies* (Grand Rapids, MI: Wm B. Eerdmans, 1973), 89, 91.

3. Wuest, *Wuest's Word Studies*, 89, 91.

Chapter 4: How God Reached Me

1. Fred Hoyle, *The Nature of the Universe* (Oxford, UK: Basil Blackwell, 1952), 109.

2. I describe and document this biblical origin and development of the scientific method in my book *Navigating Genesis* (Covina, CA: RTB Press, 2015), 29–32, 223–24.

Chapter 5: How God Readied Me

1. Hugh Ross, *Navigating Genesis* (Covina, CA: RTB Press, 2014), 25–80; Hugh Ross, *Genesis One: A Scientific Perspective*, 4th ed. (Covina, CA: Reasons to Believe, 2006).

2. Hugh Ross, *A Matter of Days*, 2nd ed. (Covina, CA: RTB Press, 2015), 139–44, 164–65.

3. Hugh Ross and Tim Callahan, *Does the Bible Have Predictive Powers?*, MP3 audio, (Covina, CA: RTB Press, 2011), shop.reasons.org/product/566/does-the-bible-have-predictive-powers-downloadable-mp3.

4. Ezekiel 34–39; Hugh Ross, "Israel: A Modern Miracle" (Covina, CA: Reasons to Believe, 1980), short paper.

Chapter 6: Readiness and "the Gift"

1. John F. MacArthur, *Charismatic Chaos* (Grand Rapids: Zondervan, 1992); Walter J. Chantry, *Signs of the Apostles: Observations on Pentecostalism Old and New* (Edinburgh: The Banner of Truth Trust, 1978); Benjamin B. Warfield, "The Cessation of the Charismata," in *Counterfeit Miracles* (New York: Charles Scribner's Sons, 1918), 1–32.

2. Wayne Grudem, *The Gift of Prophecy in the New Testament and Today* (Wheaton, IL: Crossway, 2000); D. A. Carson, *Showing the Spirit: A Theological Exposition of 1 Corinthians 12–14* (Grand Rapids, MI: Baker

Academic, 1996); Sam Storms, *The Beginner's Guide to Spiritual Gifts* (Grand Rapids, MI: Bethany House, 2013); J. Oswald Sanders, *The Holy Spirit and His Gifts* (Grand Rapids, MI: Zondervan, 1970).

3. "The Great Litany," *The (Online) Book of Common Prayer* (New York: The Church Hymnal Corporation), 149, accessed May 5, 2018, bcponline.org. These three enemies of the soul are further expounded upon in Werner Robl, "Peter Abaelard: Expositiones," (September 2002), accessed June 5, 2018, abaelard.de/050511expositio.htm; St. Thomas Aquinas, *The Summa Theologica of Saint Thomas Aquinas*, vol. 2, ed. Robert Maynard Hutchins, trans. Fathers of English Dominican Province (Chicago: Encyclopedia Britannica, 1952), 149–50, 159–62; H. J. Schroeder, "Chapter XIII: The Gift of Perseverance," *The Canons and Decrees of the Council of Trent* (Charlotte: TAN Books, 1955).

Chapter 9: Ready for the Road

1. Fazale Rana with Hugh Ross, *Who Was Adam? A Creation Model Approach to the Origin of Humanity* (Covina, CA: RTB Press, 2015).
2. James Tour, Hugh Ross, and Ben Young, *Funeral Service for Professor Richard Smalley* (November 2, 2005), mp3 audio, jmtour.com/media/smalley_funeral.mp3.

Chapter 10: Ready to Fly

1. Hartford Institute for Religion Research, "Fast Facts about American Religion: How Many Clergymen and Women Are There in the United States," (Hartford, CT: 2012), hirr.hartsem.edu/research/fastfacts/fast_facts.html.
2. A little over 5 percent of my airplane and airport conversations are with pastors and seminary professors.

Chapter 11: Always Means *Always*

1. Hugh Ross and Victor Stenger, moderated by Philip Clayton, *RTB Live!* vol. 1: *The Great Debate* (Covina, CA: Reasons to Believe, 2008), shop.reasons.org/product/332/rtb-live-volume-1-the-great-debate.

Chapter 12: Readiness Together

1. Ben Young, *Room for Doubt: How Uncertainty Can Deepen Your Faith* (Colorado Springs: David C. Cook, 2017).
2. Job 12:7–10, Psalm 19:1–2, Psalm 97:6, Psalm 104, Romans 1:19–20.
3. Two such videos that have been produced by Reasons to Believe and

filmed in front of small groups of Christians and non-Christians include *Navigating Genesis* Curriculum Kit (Covina, CA: Reasons to Believe, 2015), shop.reasons.org/product/543/navigating-genesis-curriculum-kit and *If God Made the Universe* Small Group Study (Covina, CA: Reasons to Believe, 2013), shop.reasons.org/product/542/if-god-made-the-universe-small-group-study.

4.   The class meets every Sunday from 11:00 AM to 12:30 PM at 154 W. Sierra Madre Blvd., Sierra Madre, California. The class is live-streamed at paradoxes.org. Past recordings of class episodes can be downloaded as MP3s also at paradoxes.org.

5.   Barna Group, "What Teens Aspire to Do in Life, How Churches Can Help," *Millennials & Generations* (June 14, 2011), accessed June 5, 2018, barna.com/research/what-teens-aspire-to-do-in-life-how-churches-can-help/.

6.   Barna Group, "What Teens Aspire to Do."

Chapter 13: Readiness Demeanor

1.   John S. Dickerson, *The Great Evangelical Recession: 6 Factors That Will Crash the American Church . . . and How to Prepare* (Grand Rapids, MI: Baker, 2013), 86–87.

2.   George Barna, *Revolution* (Carol Stream, IL: BarnaBooks, 2005), 32.

About the Authors

Hugh Ross is founder and president of Reasons to Believe, an organization that researches and communicates how God's revelation in the words of the Bible harmonizes with the facts of nature.

With a degree in physics from the University of British Columbia and a PhD in astronomy from the University of Toronto, he continued his research on quasars and galaxies as a postdoctoral fellow at the California Institute of Technology before transitioning to full-time ministry. In addition to founding and leading Reasons to Believe, he remains on the pastoral staff at Sierra Madre Congregational Church. His writings include journal and magazine articles and numerous books—*The Creator and the Cosmos, Why the Universe Is the Way It Is*, and *Improbable Planet*. He has spoken on hundreds of university campuses as well as at conferences and churches around the world.

He lives in Southern California with his wife, Kathy.

Kathy Ross, a native Californian, holds a master's degree in English from the University of Southern California. Soon after completing her degree she returned to USC to work in the Communications & Publications office. She also taught an evening class at Vanguard University (then Southern California College), before accepting a full-time teaching position at Pasadena City College. Then, as Hugh became more involved in ministry, Kathy joined him, heading up a women's outreach team and occasionally teaching Bible studies at their church. Together they launched Reasons to Believe. In addition to editing Hugh's books, Kathy serves as a vice president at RTB, overseeing multiple ministry departments.

Hugh and Kathy have enjoyed 40 years of marriage. They live in Southern California and have two grown sons, plus a daughter-in-law.

About Reasons to Believe

Uniquely positioned within the science-faith discussion since 1986, Reasons to Believe (RTB) communicates that science and faith are, and always will be, allies, not enemies. Distinguished for integrating science and faith respectfully and with integrity, RTB welcomes dialogue with both skeptics and believers. Addressing topics such as the origin of the universe, the origin of life, and the history and destiny of humanity, RTB's website offers a vast array of helpful resources. Through their books, blogs, podcasts, vodcasts, and speaking events, RTB scholars present powerful reasons from science to trust in the reliability of the Bible and the message it conveys about creation and redemption.

For more information, contact us via:
reasons.org
818 S. Oak Park Rd.
Covina, CA 91724
(855) REASONS / (855) 732-7667
ministrycare@reasons.org